# Getting In on the Ground Floor

# GETTING IN
# ON THE
# GROUND FLOOR

Stephen Leeb

with
Donna Leeb

*G. P. PUTNAM'S SONS / NEW YORK*

Published by G. P. Putnam's Sons, 200 Madison Avenue, New York, NY 10016
Published simultaneously in Canada by
General Publishing Co. Limited, Toronto

The text of this book is set in Baskerville.

Library of Congress Cataloging-in-Publication Data

Leeb, Stephen, date.
Getting in on the ground floor.

Includes index.
1. Speculation.    2. Stocks—United States.
I. Leeb, Donna, date.    II. Title.
HG6041.L44    1985        332.64'5        85-19374
ISBN 0-399-13091-8

Printed in the United States of America

1   2   3   4   5   6   7   8   9   10

*To our son, Timothy*
*Born under the sign of the bull*

# CONTENTS

# INTRODUCTION

Following the glorious stock market rally of August 1982, a lot of market pros were saying that it looked a lot like 1975. In January 1975, after a prolonged bear market, the market had also shot up fast and furiously on enormous volume. Both rallies came as the economy was on the verge of emerging from a severe recession. In both, the battered technology stocks were particularly big winners. It's not surprising that many analysts saw parallels and felt that the bull market of 1975–1976 was about to repeat itself.

I had a different feeling.

For some time I had been intrigued by two periods of market history: the spectacular, long-lasting bull markets that stretched from 1921 to 1929 and from 1949 to 1965. In August 1921 the Dow Jones Industrial Average stood at 63.90. By late 1929 it had climbed to 381.17, a rise of nearly 500%, and other stocks had made even more outsized gains. True, during those years there were numerous periods of market decline, periods that scared the daylights out of investors at the time. But the market always recovered. The thrust was relentlessly higher, and during those years investors made fortunes.

In the 1949–1965 period the market traced a similar pattern. That powerful long-term bull market began in June 1949 with the DJIA at 161.60. By 1965—again, with numerous intervals of decline, including the ferocious 27% plunge in 1962—the DJIA was close to 1000.

The bull market of 1975–1976 stands in obvious contrast to these two earlier periods. Stocks made substantial gains, it is true, with the DJIA rising from the mid-500s to 1000. But then the market stagnated, and it ultimately came back down as low as the 780s. The bull market of 1975–1976 was eighteen months of fun and games followed by five years of slow torture.

When stocks rallied so vigorously beginning in August 1982, I felt there were clear signs that this market resembled the powerful long-term bull markets of the 1920s and the 1949–1965 period far more than it did the relatively short-lived bull market of the 1970s. I began to study the 1920s and the 1950s and early 1960s more carefully, to try to discover what underlying factors they had in common and to see if any of those factors were present once again.

What I found was exciting. For it turned out that *the long-term bull markets of the 1920s and the 1949–1965 period were indeed characterized by a confluence of specific economic circumstances that had been in place during those years and at virtually no other moment in this century—until 1982.*

This book tells you why the 1980s are special—why I am convinced that they are akin to the two great long-term bull markets of the more distant past rather than to the ephemeral bull markets of the late 1960s and 1970s.

It outlines four specific conditions whose presence tells you that a bull market can go on and on for years— and whose faltering enables you to recognize, ahead of the crowd, that the bull is finally winding down and that it's time to get out with your profits intact.

It describes the three distinct stages that every long-term bull market goes through and tells you exactly what kinds of stocks you should be buying during each stage.

It explains how to know when a downturn in stocks is temporary and should be viewed as a fabulous buying opportunity rather than as a cause for depression.

I believe that *once you understand my four conditions for a long-term bull market and my rules for stock selection, you will be in a position to make maximum gains in stocks in the decade ahead*—a decade that I am convinced will be one of the greatest moneymaking opportunities in history. It is an opportunity that no one who has ever invested or been tempted to invest should pass up.

How high will stocks go before this bull market comes to an end? Based on an understanding of the long-term bull markets of the past, the high 3000s on the DJIA is a *conservative* estimate. My best guess is that the Dow will get close to the 4500 level before the bull expires. And that means that hundreds of other stocks will make proportionately even greater gains.

You might be asking: What is so special about the 1980s? Why did my four critical conditions suddenly come together then, after years in abeyance? What's nice about my conditions is that if you see they are in place, you really don't have to worry about why: You can simply go ahead and buy stocks and still get a good night's sleep. But it is nonetheless true that my four conditions—*which reflect the fundamental underpinnings of the economy*—do not appear and disappear at random. Their emergence in the early 1980s stemmed from several intersecting, ongoing changes that were taking place beneath the soil of American life and that finally worked themselves into the light of day. One of them is the changing nature of the American workplace. Another is a rebirth of the entrepreneurial spirit. The third is governmental deregulation, which is making the economy increasingly competitive and price-conscious. And finally there is what I call the dawning of the information age, a revolution in which the person behind a computer keyboard has become more economically significant than the man in a hard hat.

Together these trends have led to a more dynamic, competitive economy, in which inflation has been definitively tamed. The likely persistence of these trends is strong reason for believing that my conditions are not going to falter anytime soon—and that this bull market has many more years to run. Like 1921–1929 and 1949–1965, the 1980s and early 1990s are destined to go down as a period in which enormous fortunes were made in the stock market.

I hope that this book enables all of you to share in those fortunes.

This book would not have been possible without the help of many people. First and foremost is my wife, Donna Leeb, a writer and editor who is in every sense a full coauthor. We have been collaborating for many

12

years, ever since we cofounded the advisory letter *Investment Strategist* in 1979. Without her participation this book either never would have been written, or would have been much less useful.

We wish to thank our editor, Faith Sale, who with consummate skill and tact penciled out every redundancy in our manuscript, caught every mixed metaphor, and made countless valuable suggestions. For introducing us to Faith and her husband, Kirk, and for their general good offices throughout the years, we also especially want to mention Janet and David Belsky. We are grateful to Steve Kichen of *Forbes,* for his initial discussions; to Neil Barsky, for his research assistance; to Lou Barsky, for his encouragement; to Steve Quickle, for offering the opportunity to present some thoughts on secular bull markets in *City Business;* and to Felice and Edward Ross and Andrea Dalton for their indefatigable babysitting assistance. Our thanks to our staff at Money Growth Institute for typing and research assistance and in particular to Ruth Wasserman, Jean Cordero, and Kathy Farrell.

In our discussion of the dawning of the information age we relied heavily on statistical studies done by Stephen Roach of Morgan Stanley. Much of the long-term data in the chapter on money supply came from the monumental work of Milton Friedman and Anna Jacobson Schwartz, *A Monetary History of the United States: 1867–1960.*

And finally we wish to thank the subscribers to *Investment Strategist, The Speculator,* and *Penny Stock Ventures* for thinking all along that what we had to say about the market was important.

# 1

## BULLS, BEARS, AND PIGS

When the stock market opened on August 2, 1982, the Dow Jones Industrial Average was at 811.55, having declined nearly 20% since mid-1981. The country was deep in a recession, one that many considered the worst since the Great Depression. Unemployment was in double-digit territory. Reaganomics, that supposed panacea of the supply-side gang who had taken office in January 1981, seemed a dismal failure. To most investors, those who still owned stocks and those who were congratulating themselves on having gotten out of the market, the stock market appeared a lost cause.

During the next eleven days of the month the market dropped a further 34 points, bringing it to 776.92, the lowest level in more than two and a half years. But then, on Friday, August 13—a day to make the superstitious on Wall Street take to embracing black cats and walking under ladders—the market rallied over 11 points. And the following Tuesday the market took off like a Roman candle on the Fourth of July, soaring nearly 39 points on the second-highest volume in history, nearly 93 million shares. A rally of stupendous proportions had been launched. Stocks that had been lying around like sick dogs began behaving as if they had been given massive doses of megavitamins. By the end of October, for example, Informatics had gone from 10 to nearly 20, Wang Labs from the mid-20s to the low 50s. Many others, such as MCI, Tandy, Northern Telecom, and Control Data, had also nearly doubled. And the DJIA had climbed to over 1000, a stunning 29% rise in ten weeks.

Investors scrambled to get aboard. The volume of shares traded rose dramatically. Shortly before the market's surge, in the week ended July 30, for example, daily volume averaged about 46 million shares. The week ended August 30 volume averaged close to 110 million shares a day.

But many investors, amateurs and market professionals alike, had doubts as to how long the market could continue to rise. Two, five, seven years later would stocks be far higher? Or would the tide eventually turn, bringing stocks back down to the 800s or even lower?

In other words, would the bull market that began in August 1982 prove to be a short-lived *cyclical* market, one that goes up merely to turn down again shortly, like the markets of the late 1960s and the 1970s? Or would it be what is known as a *secular*—long-term—bull market, one that can last years and years and in which stocks can double and triple and then double again?

That term *secular bull market* has lately become quite fashionable in financial circles. But I suspect that most people who use it have only the haziest understanding

16

of just what a secular bull market is. They don't really know how long it can last, how high it can go, what sets it off, what could cut it short, or when it has occurred in the past. *Yet understanding secular bull markets—knowing how to recognize one and what to do about it—can be the surest means to the most enormous gains that any investor can hope to have in his or her lifetime.*

This book is about secular bull markets—and specifically about the overwhelming evidence that we are in the early stages of one right now, the infancy of what will prove to be one of the great long-term surges in history. It will give you accurate tools for recognizing such a market, knowing what kinds of stocks to buy in it, and knowing ahead of the crowd when to get out. I think this is knowledge that everyone who has ever been tempted to invest in the stock market should have.

So far in this century there have been just two true secular bull markets: from 1921 through 1929 and from 1949 through 1965.* During those golden eras the bull just didn't know the meaning of the word quit. Stocks, in defiance of gravity and the ever-dwindling crowd of skeptics, kept making outsized leaps upward. Whenever it seemed as if the bull must finally be getting winded, he would burst forth with renewed energy, and stocks would start climbing again—until finally, after many years, the bull did collapse, mortally wounded by forces outside his control. But during the years in which he reigned, investors made fortunes.

By contrast, all the other bull markets of this century

---

*Actually, one might also include the period from 1933 to 1937, which is a special case that can be viewed as a "mini secular bull market." As you'll see in chapter 7, my conditions were in place during those years as well.

17

have been cyclical affairs, lasting only a couple of years. While the secular bull markets were freewheeling trips into outer space, these cyclical markets were elevator rides, remaining within predictable limits. While it was certainly possible to make money in the market during those periods, the opportunities for giant-sized gains were far less and, even more important, the risks were far greater.

It is easy in retrospect to tell which markets are cyclical and which secular. But when you are going through the day-to-day fluctuations of the market it is far more difficult. When stocks are going up, how do you know whether to take a profit or to hold on for much bigger gains ahead? And when stocks are going down—as they will for months at a time even in the strongest bull market—how can you tell if you should get out, grateful for only a small loss, or hang on in the conviction that the market will soon be winging its way up once again?

Anyone who follows stocks knows that at any given moment market pros can't even agree as to whether the market is in a bull or a bear phase. When stocks are rising, there are always people around who insist that it is nothing more than a bull trap in a bear market. And when stocks are falling, some will argue that it is merely a temporary "correction" in a basically bullish trend.

The difference between a bull market and a bear market is, certainly, important—but, when it comes to scoring big, that difference is less significant than the difference between a *cyclical* market and a *secular* market. And that is a distinction that most market pros fail even to understand, much less apply. Yet once you can grasp

18

this distinction, and know how to tell which kind of market you're in, cyclical or secular, you have it within your reach to make a fortune in stocks—if you're lucky enough to be around during a secular bull market.

And that is the crux of the matter. It is my contention that *the bull market that began in August 1982 will prove to be the third great secular bull market of this century,* lasting well into the 1990s and sweeping stocks into new stratospheres. I'm not saying this out of mere wishful thinking, for there are definite signs that this market is totally different from the cyclical markets of the late 1960s and 1970s, and that it is akin to the secular bull markets of the 1921–1929 and the 1949–1965 periods.

If I am right, then this is the time to buy stocks hand over fist and hold on to them regardless of any temporary setbacks. And if you're fretting that you're still on the sidelines, don't worry: One of the most remarkable things about a secular bull market is that *you can get in at any point and still make a fortune.*

To help you grasp more fully the crucial difference between secular and cyclical markets, consider the following three morality tales.

## Tale No. 1:
## Peter the Premature

It's mid-August 1962, and Peter has just heard from his broker about a new stock. This is actually the last thing he wants to know about, for his portfolio has taken a tremendous beating between January and June, a

19

period in which the Dow Jones Industrial Average plunged more than 25%. But lately the market has shown some signs of life, and once a player, always a player. Peter resists the urge to buy immediately, but he watches the stock. Four weeks later it has climbed about 10%. Maybe there is something there after all.

Peter takes a closer look at the company. It is a rapidly growing drug manufacturer. But not entirely undiscovered—it is selling at more than 50 times earnings. Okay, so even if he won't be first on his block to own it, he may still be able to make a good buck. Peter decides to take a shot and buys 100 shares, for about $3600.

Fall follows summer, and Peter's stock follows the temperature: It declines. In fact, four months later it has lost one-third of its value, trading near 24. Peter is tempted to get out. But, he tells himself, after all, nothing has really changed with the company. Earnings are still growing rapidly, and what's more, the economy appears to be on firm footing. Peter sticks with it.

A good thing. By August 1963 the stock is trading at 96, and Peter has made about $6000, in those days enough to pay for two years at a good private college. When you have two teenage children, the temptation to lock in the profit is great. Peter takes another look at the company. Profits in 1963 will likely be quadruple those of 1962. Great growth—but how long can it continue? Peter sells.

Poor Peter. Two and a half years later the stock is selling at 120. And this is *after* a 3:1 split followed by a 2:1 split—an effective price of $720 a share. If Peter had held on, his $3600 investment would have turned into

$72,000. The stock? It was Syntex, one of the original marketers of birth-control pills.

## Tale No. 2:
## Frank the Frustrated

Now let's jump ahead about fifteen years. It's summer 1978, and Frank is looking for an exciting stock. He calls his broker, who, not surprisingly, has several ideas. One of these strikes Frank's fancy, a company with an excellent growth history and prospects for more of the same. Profits in 1978 will probably be 50% above 1977 results, and growth is expected to be around 30% a year through at least the early 1980s. Concepts like these made millionaires out of those who bought stocks like Syntex in the 1960s. Frank plunges in and buys 1000 shares at $30 a share.

One week later the stock is trading at 35. Frank's on cloud nine. Should he buy more? Well, maybe an additional 100 shares. This could be the chance for a really big score. Poor Frank. October 1979 was to become known as the October massacre, and Frank's stock was one of the worst victims. By mid-December, instead of a big score, Frank was sitting with a stock worth less than half its original value.

Frank is no quitter. He sticks it out, and by mid-1979 the stock is trading above 40. But, he reasons, he hasn't gone through all that agony just for a 5-to-10-point gain, especially since the company's earnings are still growing rapidly. As it turns out, he should have sold. October 1979 became known as the second October massacre, and Frank's stock again was among those hardest hit, reaching a low in the mid-20s before firming.

The next several years are frustrating. The stock makes about five round trips from the upper teens to the low 30s. True, profits continue to grow—Frank had been right on that score. But where it really counted, the stock price, he was wrong. Eventually, totally frustrated, he sold at 20. The stock? Bally Manufacturing, maker of slot machines and other leisure-time products.

# Tale No. 3:
# Larry the Loser

It's summer 1971, and the stock market has been advancing for almost a year, though lately it has been showing some signs of weakness. Since May 1969 the Dow has risen from the low 600s to the high 800s, occasionally poking its head above 900. Larry, a few years out of college, is married, and he and his wife, Jane, have a young child. Everyone he talks to seems to be making money in the market. Hard work and gifts from parents have resulted in their $15,000 savings account. Jane is conservative; she wants nothing to do with the stock market. So what if someone else is making money? Can't Larry just be content with what they have? In a couple of years, if they work hard, they'll be in a position to buy a house, she says—let's not take any chances.

But Larry can't stand the idea that all his friends are making a killing in the market. If things go as he expects, he'll have the money to buy a house, not to mention a car and a country club membership, in well under two years. He takes the $15,000 out of their savings account and deposits it with a broker.

Which stocks should he buy? He wants to go with something he's familiar with. He picks a company that's a household name and is selling for $150 a share. His friends assure him that although growth has slowed a bit in recent years, the stock price has been going up steadily and the future is as bright as ever. With his $15,000, Larry buys 100 shares.

From the start things go wrong. Over the next six months the stock declines to about 100. So much for getting the house sooner, not to mention the car and club. His broker and friends tell him to sit tight—prospects for the company are still bright. Jane wants him to sell and take the loss as a once-and-for-all lesson to leave the market alone: Larry's friends may have made money in stocks, Jane has not. But Larry holds on, and over the next six months the stock rallies back to the 140 area. His patience has apparently paid off. Now it is only a matter of time before the stock reaches 200 and even 250. The house, the car, and the club are finally within reach.

But this is not a story with a happy ending. Over the next twelve months the stock slides steadily, finally reaching a low of 14 in September 1974. Larry hasn't stayed for quite the whole horrible downside ride—he sold at 20 in August 1974. His $15,000 had turned into $2000. Fortunately, he was still young and had a good job. To the best of our knowledge, however, Larry's purchase of Polaroid in 1971 was his first and last venture in the stock market.

\*　　\*　　\*

These three stories illustrate important segments of stock market history, and some of the opportunities and pitfalls of secular and cyclical markets. In the simplest terms, cyclical means relatively short term and secular relatively long term. But there is more to it than that. A cyclical trend is really no trend at all. It is a cycle that starts at one place and goes up or down but eventually comes back to where it started. It is almost like a random fluctuation around a line. It is a reflection that the basic factors influencing the trend are not really changing in any significant way.

By contrast, *a secular trend occurs when important fundamental underpinnings shift in a dramatic fashion in such a way that the trend becomes self-sustaining.* A secular trend can go on and on for years, with just minor setbacks that are quickly made up.

It's really not so complicated. Suppose you know someone who has been married and divorced three times. Next thing you know, you get an engraved wedding invitation in the mail: He's ready to try again. And this time he swears it's the real thing—it will last forever. But will it? Understandably you're skeptical, not to mention a bit tired of buying him wedding presents. But there is a chance that he is right and that this time the marriage will survive. Whether it does will probably depend on whether there have been fundamental changes in him. If he is essentially the same person as when he got married the first time, you wouldn't give the fourth wife's chances a prayer. His marriage will likely be of brief duration, and his love life will continue to be characterized by cyclical affairs—short-term events that go nowhere.

24

But now suppose that after his third marriage collapsed he went into therapy and came to grips with a lifelong fear of commitment. That might represent a fundamental change—a secular change. And if so, just maybe this marriage will last. His love life may be about to begin a secular uptrend.

It may seem far-fetched to compare someone's love life with the stock market, but it's not. In both love and the market the relevant questions are the same. You have to know who and where you are and how you got there. You have to be able to distinguish the transient from the permanent—the cyclical from the secular.

Now you can see where Peter, Frank, and Larry went wrong. Peter and Larry both made the mistake of misdiagnosing a secular trend. They failed to recognize that important fundamental shifts had taken place— changes that would trigger a long-term uptrend, in Peter's case, and a long-term downtrend, in Larry's case. Peter sold too soon in a secular bull market. He figured that growth had to slow eventually. But in a secular bull market, growth can go on and on. Larry's mistake was even worse. He bought near the start of a long-term bear market and then kept telling himself that the market was certain to turn around soon. He didn't know enough to take his loss and get out.

Frank, on the other hand, kept looking for a secular trend that never developed. He was caught right smack in the middle of the meandering, frustrating cyclical market of the late 1970s, but he kept thinking that he was in the exciting long-term bull market of the early 1960s. If he had recognized that he was in a cyclical market, he would have known to take short-term profits

25

and to move in and out of stocks. Instead, he tried to apply a buy-and-hold strategy that is appropriate only in secular bull markets.

It should now be clearer why cyclical and secular are such important concepts—and why some bull markets have better potential for profit than others. In cyclical markets you tend to play for smaller gains, though it's possible to end up doing very well. It's like playing golf by chipping your ball from the tee to the green, a few yards at a time. You can get there, but it tends to be hard work.

Making money in a secular bull market is hitting out that long, perfect, straight, 300-yard drive. In secular markets you can be greedy—nay, gluttonous! A common Wall Street adage has it that bulls can make money, bears can make money, but pigs almost always lose. Not so. In secular bull markets, pigs make fortunes.

Look at the chart of Syntex (Figure 1-1). If you had been lucky enough to buy at the bottom, you might have watched it double or triple and—like Peter—told yourself, "Let's not be a pig about it," and sold. Like Peter, you'd never stop regretting it. *In secular bull markets you can buy stocks even after they have doubled and tripled and still make a fortune.* Syntex was far from being the only such meteoric performer in the early 1960s. Texas Instruments, for example, in mid-1958 was trading at 35; by early 1959 the stock had shot up to over 85, and, despite several brief but scary corrections, by the end of 1959 had reached a high of more than 190. The story of Fairchild Camera is even more dramatic. In mid-1958 the stock was trading in the mid-20s. By the end of the year it had touched 60, and by mid-1959 it had soared

26

to over 200. Anyone who had sold there would have been happy—for a short time, anyway. The stock tumbled to around 125. But by the end of the year Fairchild was trading at an effective price of 280 a share. Look at Figure 1-2, "Big Winners in the Second Secular Bull Market," for other mouth-watering examples.

In the bear market of the 1970s, Polaroid, again, was far from being the only big loser. As Figure 1-3 shows, the bluest of all the blue chips, IBM, traded at a high of over 91 in 1973. By October 1974 the stock had skidded to below 40 a share. The drop in General Motors was even more severe. From a high of over 90 in 1971, it sank to below 30 in the depths of the 1974 bear market. Other stocks suffered equally sickening slides.

As for the cyclical market that played havoc with Frank's hopes, Figure 1-4, the DJIA, shows vividly that over the fifteen-year period between 1966 and 1981 this best-known market average went virtually nowhere, as did most of the stocks that made up the average, and a good many other stocks as well.

These examples, and the stories of Peter, Frank, and Larry, should whet your appetite for a secular bull market; after all, wouldn't it be nice if you could find a few Syntexes of your own? If you could buy stocks and serenely hold on, knowing that any downturn will prove temporary and simply represents an opportunity to accumulate more shares at a lower price?

Moreover, from what I've said so far you should be getting the idea that if I am right, and we are in a secular bull market today, it must be because—as with the hypothetical multiple bridegroom—there have been enormously significant changes in the fundamental un-

27

## FIGURE 1-1   SYNTEX: 1961–1966

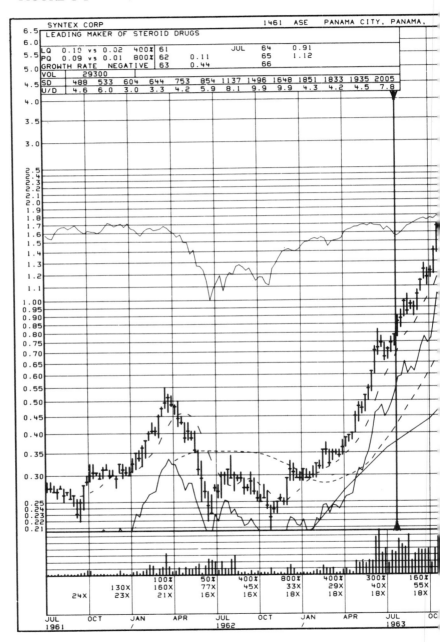

Courtesy of Daily Graphs

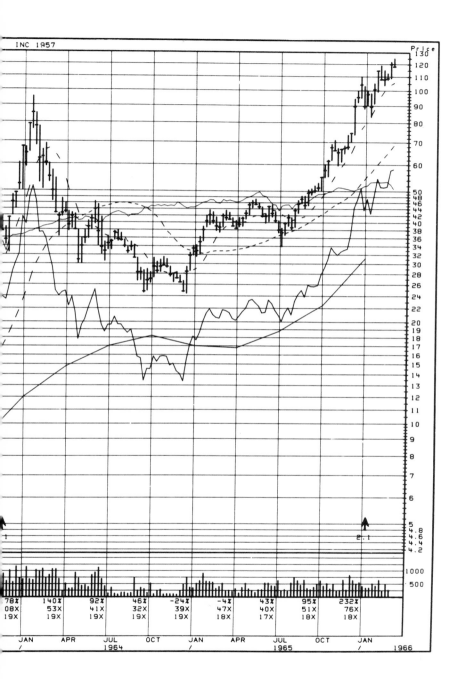

FIGURE 1-2

# BIG WINNERS IN THE SECOND SECULAR BULL MARKET

| Stock | Start of Advance | | | End of Advance | | | |
|---|---|---|---|---|---|---|---|
| | Year | Qtr | Price | Year | Qtr | Price* | % Gain |
| Addressograph | 1953 | 4 | 9 | 1961 | 4 | 110 | 1122 |
| American Machine | 1956 | 2 | 6 | 1961 | 2 | 63 | 950 |
| Black & Decker | 1953 | 4 | 3 | 1965 | 4 | 43 | 1333 |
| Bristol-Myers | 1954 | 3 | 2 | 1965 | 4 | 50 | 2400 |
| Caterpillar Tractor | 1954 | 1 | 4 | 1965 | 4 | 54 | 1250 |
| Coca-Cola | 1957 | 4 | 8 | 1965 | 4 | 45 | 463 |
| Crown Cork | 1958 | 1 | 3 | 1966 | 2 | 66 | 2100 |
| Del Monte | 1953 | 3 | 5 | 1961 | 4 | 37 | 640 |
| Delta Airlines | 1962 | 2 | 3 | 1966 | 2 | 44 | 1367 |
| Eastman Kodak | 1953 | 3 | 5 | 1966 | 2 | 70 | 1300 |
| Emerson Electric | 1955 | 2 | 2 | 1965 | 4 | 31 | 1450 |
| Fairchild Camera | 1958 | 4 | 4 | 1960 | 3 | 64 | 1500 |
| Fairchild Camera | 1964 | 4 | 15 | 1966 | 1 | 140 | 833 |
| General Cigar | 1954 | 2 | 6 | 1964 | 3 | 78 | 1200 |
| Greyhound | 1954 | 1 | 2 | 1964 | 2 | 31 | 1450 |
| IBM | 1954 | 1 | 8 | 1965 | 4 | 180 | 2150 |
| Motorola | 1958 | 2 | 16 | 1966 | 2 | 230 | 1338 |
| Polaroid | 1955 | 4 | 2 | 1966 | 3 | 85 | 4150 |
| Scott Paper | 1953 | 1 | 8 | 1961 | 4 | 50 | 525 |
| Smith Kline | 1955 | 1 | 7 | 1965 | 2 | 87 | 1143 |
| Texas Inst. | 1956 | 1 | 4 | 1960 | 2 | 102 | 2450 |
| Universal Leaf | 1954 | 1 | 2 | 1961 | 4 | 27 | 1250 |
| Xerox | 1958 | 1 | 3 | 1966 | 2 | 270 | 8900 |

*Where necessary adjusted for stock splits (as of 1969).

30

FIGURE 1-3

# BIG LOSERS IN THE CYCLICAL MARKET OF THE 1970S

| Stock | Start of Decline | | | End of Decline | | | |
|---|---|---|---|---|---|---|---|
| | *Year* | *Qtr* | *Price* | *Year* | *Qtr* | *Price* | *% Loss* |
| Burroughs | 1973 | 4 | 126 | 1981 | 4 | 30 | −76 |
| Cluett, Peabody | 1968 | 3 | 36 | 1974 | 4 | 3 | −92 |
| Coca-Cola | 1973 | 1 | 75 | 1974 | 4 | 22 | −71 |
| Collins & Aikman | 1972 | 2 | 16 | 1974 | 4 | 2 | −88 |
| Control Data | 1969 | 1 | 80 | 1974 | 4 | 5 | −94 |
| Di Giorgio | 1969 | 3 | 28 | 1974 | 4 | 3 | −89 |
| Eastman Kodak | 1973 | 1 | 101 | 1980 | 2 | 29 | −71 |
| General Motors | 1971 | 1 | 91 | 1974 | 4 | 29 | −68 |
| Gerber Products | 1971 | 3 | 24 | 1974 | 3 | 4 | −83 |
| Gulton Ind. | 1969 | 1 | 40 | 1974 | 4 | 2 | −95 |
| IBM | 1973 | 1 | 91 | 1974 | 3 | 38 | −58 |
| Johnson Controls | 1972 | 1 | 20 | 1974 | 4 | 4 | −80 |
| Lilly, Eli | 1973 | 2 | 93 | 1977 | 4 | 33 | −65 |
| Nat'l Semi | 1980 | 4 | 17 | 1982 | 3 | 4 | −76 |
| Penney, J.C. | 1973 | 1 | 101 | 1980 | 4 | 20 | −80 |
| Polaroid | 1972 | 2 | 150 | 1974 | 4 | 14 | −91 |
| Sears | 1973 | 1 | 62 | 1980 | 4 | 14 | −77 |
| Syntex | 1973 | 4 | 32 | 1977 | 4 | 8 | −75 |
| Vernitron | 1969 | 1 | 41 | 1974 | 4 | 1 | −98 |
| Westinghouse | 1972 | 2 | 28 | 1974 | 4 | 4 | −86 |
| Xerox | 1972 | 3 | 172 | 1982 | 2 | 27 | −84 |

derpinnings, in this case the economic underpinnings. And this is precisely right. Secular bull markets, while they always take the great majority of investors by surprise, don't happen out of the blue. They aren't accidents. They are born out of *major realignments of economic forces.* Whatever the beliefs of pure market technicians—who will tell you to disregard everything but the behavior of the market itself—the market reflects and is affected by the surrounding economic environment. Tax policies, interest rates, regulatory policies, and a host of other complex, interrelated factors influence whether or not a secular bull market is in the cards. When these factors coalesce in a favorable fashion, the secular bull is unleashed. When they fail to come together, or move out of place, then the secular bull is doomed.

FIGURE 1-4

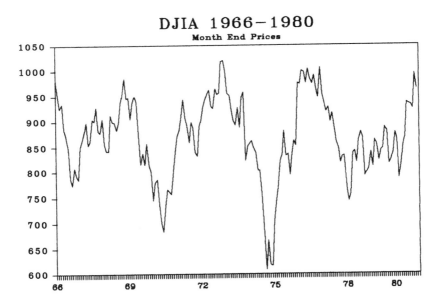

DJIA 1966-1980
Month End Prices

32

This may already sound excruciatingly complicated. After all, if the market is affected by such a mass of economic and even political factors, how can the average investor hope to have enough time and knowledge to make sense of it all? It would seem to be a full-time job that requires at the very least a Ph.D. in economics, statistics, mathematics, and political science.

But fortunately, recognizing a secular bull market is not all that difficult. I have taken a close look at the secular bull markets of the past—analyzing not just how stocks themselves behaved during those periods but, more important, *isolating precisely which factors were responsible for the secular bull's emergence.* And I discovered a rather remarkable fact: There are just four relatively simple conditions—four economic relationships—that prevail whenever the secular bull is in place and that wane just as the secular bull is about to expire. These four conditions in and of themselves summarize and synthesize all the relevant economic data that bear upon the long-term direction of stocks.

## The Four Conditions

*Condition No. 1:* Real growth must be greater than inflation. In the recent past, inflation has time and again short-circuited economic growth and thrown the bull for a loop. The result has been the cyclical boom-bust economies and stock markets of the late 1960s and 1970s. But inflation doesn't always have to be deadly. Knowing how to recognize when it is sufficiently under control so as to be

33

compatible with a sustained bull market is critical to getting in at the early stages of a major bull move. The criterion of real growth enables you to determine when inflation is just a minor irritation and when it is a serious problem.

**Condition No. 2:** Bond yields must be twice the inflation rate. This is a simple but highly accurate indicator that, like the first condition, lets you know when economic growth is sustainable.

**Condition No. 3:** Short-term interest rates must be lower than long-term rates. If you see short-term rates start to overtake long-term rates, you know the bull is in trouble.

**Condition No. 4:** The money supply must be growing at a time when the other three conditions are also falling into line. If money growth declines for any significant period of time, a bull market is doomed.


If you understand and can apply my four conditions, you don't have to worry about anything else. When you see that they are operative, you know the odds are extremely good that we have embarked upon a secular bull market. Ignore whatever your neighbors, relatives, and the financial writers may be saying, for secular bull markets tend to be born when gloom-and-doomers are in the ascendancy. Buy and hold stocks for all you're worth. When you see one or more of the four conditions begin to falter, it's time to get cautious, even if everyone else is getting more and more euphoric.

Anyone who had mastered the application of the four conditions would have realized that just around the time the first secular bull market was being launched, the market was entering an entirely different phase from the cyclical markets of the past. Equally important, that same investor would have known *before* the crash of 1929 that the secular bull was expiring and that it was time to get out of stocks and would have been one of the few people around to weather the crash with all his or her gains intact.

In 1933, a knowledge of these conditions would have gotten our investor back into stocks in time for the mini secular bull market that began that year. And it would have propelled him or her into the market in spring 1949, just as the second great secular bull market of the century was getting off the ground.

It is a striking fact that these four conditions fell into place in the early 1980s and have remained in place ever since. This is extremely strong evidence that *the bull market that began in 1982 will prove to be a long-term affair which will sweep stocks far higher than most investors dare dream.* It is a strong sign that this is the time to think big—a time to ride out any short-term downturn and to let your piggish instincts run riot.

If I'm right, and we are in the early stages of a third great secular bull market, how high will stocks go? Based on my study of past secular bull markets, I think that the current market is almost certain to reach well into the 3000s on the DJIA and that it may well go as high as 4500. And this means that a multitude of smaller growth stocks could do even better, soaring not just 100% but 500%, 600%, even 1000%.

I want to make one final point in this chapter, and you should already be getting the idea: My four conditions are not gimmicks. They are not akin to technical indicators, which simply assert that if one thing happens—if, for example, the market crosses a precise point at a precise time—something else will happen, without any clear explanation as to why this should be so.

The four conditions are statements about *what ultimately drives the market*. If you follow the explanations in the succeeding chapters, you will not only know how to recognize whether or not the market is in a long-term secular uptrend and how to spot long before others when the uptrend is ending. *You will have a far greater understanding than before of exactly what makes the market tick.* And this understanding will stand you in good stead in *any* kind of market, helping you for the rest of your life to see through the claims and predictions made by the market gurus and to evaluate them for what they are worth. In short, you can become your own guru.

## 2

# GROWTH IS THE KEY

When my son Timothy was born, one of my favorite gifts that he received was a royal-blue bathrobe labeled 3T. That, I learned, meant that it was for a three-year-old toddler. Obviously, the robe was far too big for Timothy at the time, but the reason it delighted me so was that it vividly brought home the amazing fact that the tiny helpless infant in my arms would grow to be a little boy running around after his bath—an enchanting prospect.

The stock market is also beguiled by thoughts of growth. And *all four of my basic conditions are tools—the most accurate ones I know of—for predicting economic growth.* Or, to be more specific, they are ways of predicting whether economic growth is sustainable. For the single most important thing to realize about the market is that it thrives on prospects of sustainable growth. When the economy is on a sustained growth path, with any downturn representing only a brief interruption, the secular bull can thrive. When the prospects for growth are limited, when the economy itself is on a cyclical path, no uptrend in stocks can last for long.

This may sound simple, but determining if the market is in a long-term uptrend is something that economists have had amazingly little success at doing. In fact, they have a notoriously poor record in any sort of forecasting. Remember the red-hot recovery of 1983, in which the economy zoomed ahead at a 6.4% clip? In 1982 most economists were predicting a growth rate of less than 2%. And it isn't difficult to realize that the difference between 2% and 6.4% is more than simply 4.4 percentage points: It is the difference between rising and falling unemployment and has major policy implications for all levels of government. If underestimating the extent of good news is reproachable, the failure to anticipate bad news is even worse. In 1982 the economy by many measures experienced its worst recession since the 1930s, yet in mid-1981 the consensus forecast among economists was for solid economic growth the following year. Nobel Prize–winning economist Paul Samuelson has quipped that the stock market has predicted ten of the last three recessions. Perhaps. But economists predicted *none* of them.

My conditions, which I've developed by isolating the behavior of key economic variables during the secular bull markets of the past, have an excellent record as guides to the sustainability of economic growth. But first let's see why understanding growth is so central to understanding the market itself.

Let's ask a basic question: Why does a share of stock cost what it does? Suppose a company is trading at $20 a share and has 1 million shares outstanding. This means that the market values the company at $20 million. But what exactly does this tell you? You might reasonably assume that it implies that the company has a book value (assets less liabilities) of $20 million. But that isn't so. In fact, at any given time only a handful of companies are likely to be trading at their book value.

Not that book value isn't a helpful concept. It is an accounting term that is useful in evaluating stocks in much the same way, say, that weight and height are useful in evaluating a person's athletic ability. Height and weight are objective, measurable, characteristics that make it possible to compare two different individuals. Similarly, book value per share is an objective measure that makes it possible to compare two companies, using the same yardstick. But as may be the case with height and weight, what really counts is how book value correlates with other variables.

In general, for example, the taller a person is, the more likely that he or she will be a good basketball player. With a company, the greater the book value, the more likely that the stock price will be high. But not all short people are poor basketball players—remember 5'8" Calvin Murphy—and not every seven-footer is an NBA star. Coordination and general athletic ability play a critical role. If you see that a short person is a better basketball player than a tall one, you can rightly assume that the short person has greater athletic gifts.

With a stock, *growth prospects* are the equivalent to athletic ability. When you see two stocks that have the same book value per share, and one is trading at 20 and the other at 30, you can assume that the $30 stock has more exciting growth prospects. This is what investors are paying up for. It is *perceived growth potential* that explains a stock's price at any given moment.

Examples of stocks trading well above book value, at what is called a *premium* to book, exist in every market. In strong economies, when investors expect a lot of companies to grow rapidly, a great many companies will trade well above book. Even in recessions, when stocks in general are depressed, some companies, those for which expectations of growth are high, will do the same.

A classic example is Intel, the leading maker of microprocessors, those computers-on-a-chip that make it possible for everything from cars to dishwashers to be computer-run. In 1973, when the market was faltering badly, Intel was trading at a staggering 14 times book value. Investors, perceiving that computers would become more and more important in every area of modern life, and that microprocessors would be at the heart of every computer, expected massive growth from Intel. They were right: In 1975 profits jumped fourfold, and by 1983 the company's book value was more than 50 times what it had been a decade earlier.

Sometimes you can get the best of both worlds. My favorite example is National Medical Enterprises. In the early and middle 1970s, no one was paying much attention to the fact that America was starting to age and that this demographic trend would result in a need for more health-care facilities. As a result, investor-owned hospital chains such as National Medical Enterprises were trading at well below book, at what is called a *discount* to book. In 1973, for example, the company traded as low as 30% of its book value, and this despite the fact that profits since 1969 had grown without inter-

40

ruption from $.06 a share to $16 a share. Growth was there, and so were prospects of future growth, but investors, for a while, were looking elsewhere.

In the decade that followed, National Medical Enterprises, sublimely indifferent to the cold shoulder it was getting from investors, continued to show rapid growth in earnings. Finally investors caught on to the fact that the company could be expected to continue to benefit from ongoing demographic changes and the insufficiency of public health-care facilities. Expectations of growth caught up with growth, and the stock price zoomed from 60 cents a share in 1973 to a high of over 32 in 1983, for a stupendous 5300% gain. This compares with a 3000% gain in Intel over the same period. And this points up one important lesson about growth: While it always pays to recognize growth, it is particularly profitable to do so before anyone else does. If you can find a company that is trading below book value but whose growth prospects are super, over the long run you will make a fortune.

The experience of Storage Technology, a manufacturer of computer peripheral equipment, illustrates in a different fashion what changing expectations can mean in terms of a stock's valuation. In 1976 Storage Tech already had an established growth record. Profits had expanded nearly threefold in the preceding four years. But investors felt that this growth might not be maintainable, as Storage Tech was competing against the biggest of the big, IBM. And the stock spent the year fluctuating very narrowly on both sides of book value.

Over the next two years growth started to accelerate. By 1978 profits jumped to $1.15 a share from $.42 in 1976. Even more important, the company had established what investors perceived to be a niche in the peripheral equipment market. In those days IBM was still hampered by an antitrust suit and was content to leave some areas alone, such as the one that Storage Technology appeared to occupy. As a result, the stock at its high in 1978 traded at more than a 300% premium to book. Growth continued through 1981, and investors' expectations remained more or less constant, with the result that in that year the stock still commanded a nearly 200% premium to book.

The following year the company was hurt by the weak economy, and earnings declined. But even more important, at the start of 1982 the government dropped its antitrust case against IBM. Storage Technology's niche was no longer secure. By the end of the year the stock was trading just about level with book. Many analysts were recommending it as a tech stock on the bargain counter, one that investors had overlooked in the early stages of the 1982 bull market. But investors were right not to pay up for future growth, for growth was not there. Profits turned to losses in 1983 and 1984, and by mid-1984 the stock was trading at about a 40% discount to book value, a clear sign of increasing investor wariness. And there were no happy surprises; by the end of 1984 the company had gone bankrupt.

These examples all demonstrate that it is expectations of growth that drive the market (though, as with National Medical Enterprises, the market can occasionally be nearsighted, creating exceptional opportunities for farsighted investors). *The market is future-oriented. It cares only about what a company will do, not what it has done.*

Or rather, it is interested in past growth only as a guide to possible future growth. It is like someone who is looking for a job. An impressive résumé counts only if there is reason to believe that the person will perform as well in a new job as in the past. If meanwhile something has happened to make that doubtful—if the applicant has developed a drinking problem, for example—the résumé would go out the window. The market, too, doesn't hand out merit awards for past performance; it is interested only in what lies ahead.

And here we come to the heart of what the market wants: not just future growth but *sustained future growth.* The market has no use for a company that will show earnings growth for a year or two more and then falter. If it is already in the cards that a company's growth can't be sustained for the foreseeable future, the market will lose interest and the stock price will sag.

Again, the analogy of a relationship may shed some light. Suppose you're single and getting a bit lonely. One by one, all your friends have been getting married and having families, and you feel that life is passing you by. Just at this vulnerable moment you meet someone wonderful, and for both of you it's love at first sight. Before you even know each other's astrological signs you're planning a Hawaiian honeymoon. As far as you're concerned, your future is settled. But then suppose that you could look into the future and learn that in two years your beloved would unaccountably leave you for someone else. Chances are you would immediately start haunting the singles bars again, hoping to meet someone else. Even though your relationship has two years left to run, in your head it is already over.

\*     \*     \*

So far, in talking about expectations for sustained growth, I have been talking in terms of the growth prospects of individual companies. But while some companies, like Intel in the 1970s, may buck the economic tide, most of them ebb and flow with the fortunes of the economy as a whole. This is true almost by definition: The economy is the sum total of the multitude of individual companies. If overall economic growth is strong, it is a reflection of strong growth on the part of many companies. If growth is weak or negative, it means that the great majority of businesses are doing poorly.

But there is more to it than that. When the overall economy is thriving, opportunities are greater all around; growth begets growth. As existing companies expand, they need to order more goods and services from other companies, which in turn help support the growth of still other companies. Of critical importance, conditions are ripe for new companies to get off the ground successfully, and these start-ups can maintain startling high growth rates for many years.

Secular bull markets arise out of prospects for sustained growth of the economy as a whole. When the economy appears strong as far as the eye can see, the earnings growth prospects for the mass of individual companies will also be strong. Investors will reward such prospects by buying stocks, and they will be rewarded in turn by rising stock prices. The phrase may be unwieldy but the thought is precise: *Secular bull markets are characterized by the fulfilled expectations of sustained economic growth.*

\*     \*     \*

44

Predicting a secular bull market in the 1980s and early 1990s, then, is equivalent to asserting that economic growth will continue throughout those years. But regardless of what my four conditions might say, aren't I ignoring one critical factor with the potential to derail economic growth? What about the huge federal budget deficit that has everyone so alarmed?

In 1984 the federal budget deficit—the difference between what Washington takes in and what it spends in a given fiscal year—was $175 billion, with a $200 billion deficit projected for 1985. These numbers sound appalling, and it's not surprising that so many people believe that this enormous debt could sink all of us.

But the deficit isn't the problem everyone thinks it is. To explain why, let's bring the issue down to a more human scale. Suppose you have a friend named Lou, who is in his mid-forties. Lou is a cautious, conservative sort of a fellow, the kind who has worked for the same company for fifteen years and who leaves tips of precisely 15% in restaurants. Not surprisingly, Lou has never been tempted to borrow money.

But one day Lou wakes up feeling that his life is a bit flat. Walking home from work, as usual he passes the Porsche showroom. He is seized by an uncontrollable desire to own one of the shiny sleek cars. Next thing you know Lou has arranged to borrow $30,000 and is the happy if somewhat dazed owner of a forest-green sports car. And for the first time in his life Lou is in debt. Since his income is $90,000, he is, in fact, in debt to the tune of 33⅓% of his income.

Now suppose you have another friend, Jake. Jake also earns $90,000. But there any similarities to Lou end. Jake is a chronic spendthrift. He owns two cars and has just bought a condominium in Florida. He also owns five credit cards, which he uses liberally. Altogether he has piled up debts of $180,000.

One night a year ago, Jake woke up in a cold sweat just thinking about how much he owed. Despite his free-spending past, Jake is not compulsively self-destructive. He decided that for the next twelve months he would not borrow a cent more.

Let's compare Lou and Jake. Which one do you think is in better shape financially? Without hesitation you would answer Lou. His debt amounts to only one-third of his income, while Jake's is twice his income. It is irrelevant that Lou has recently incurred a debt of $30,000, while Jake has borrowed nothing in the current year. Lou still comes out ahead. It's obvious.

And Lou *is* better off. Yet if you talked about each one's finances in the same terms that everyone discusses government finances—in terms of deficits—you would have given the opposite answer. For Lou has a deficit of $30,000, fully one-third his income, while Jake has no deficit at all.

You should be getting the sense of a simple but crucial distinction—between what can be termed the debt ratio and what can be called the deficit ratio. A *debt* ratio is defined as total debt divided by income—for Lou, 33⅓%, for Jake, 200%. A *deficit* ratio is debt taken on in a particular year divided by income—for Lou, still 33⅓%, for Jake, 0%. This is a distinction that bears directly on the current economic situation.

In 1984 the federal government had a deficit ratio of about 6%. That is, the amount of additional debt acquired during that year—roughly $175 billion—was equivalent to about 6% of the country's Gross National

Product. A figure of 6% is high by historical standards, there is no doubt about it. In fact, you would have to go back as far as the war years of the 1940s to find higher deficit ratios.

But, as we saw, what really counts in assessing financial well-being is not the deficit ratio but the debt ratio. In 1984 our debt ratio was approximately 43%—i.e., total government debt divided by GNP was 43%. And by historical standards 43% is not a particularly high number. In fact, it is below the sixty-year average of the debt ratio, which is approximately 50%.

Even more to the point, at the start of the great postwar secular bull market, the debt ratio was above 100%, more than twice as high as today's. And for almost the entire sixteen years of that bull market the debt ratio remained higher than the current figure, although during those years it declined considerably (the debt ratio also declined during the 1921–1929 secular bull market). By contrast, during the erratic mid-1960s, 1970s, and early 1980s the debt ratio was lower than it had been during the preceding years, when the bull was in command. Obviously, *relatively high debt ratios can go hand in hand with long-term bull markets*. And since debt ratios are more important than deficit ratios, the inescapable implication is that fairly high deficit ratios are also no bar to the secular bull.

It is possible, however, that a *rising* debt ratio is incompatible with a secular bull market—after all, during both secular bull markets of the past the debt ratio *declined*. And here you can raise an entirely valid point. Suppose, you say, that Lou, after buying his Porsche, bought an expensive Manhattan co-op, and then a sable coat for his wife. Borrowing became a habit rather

47

than a one-time impulse. In that case the mounting deficits would quickly nudge his debt ratio higher and higher. So even if the debt ratio is what ultimately counts, deficits also count because of their impact on the debt ratio.

This is true. And in theory, if the U.S. were to continue to rack up ever larger deficits, the debt ratio *could* start to climb. But I think there is virtually no chance that this will happen. In fact, the debt ratio is almost certain to decline—giving us the best of both worlds, a debt ratio that is relatively low to start with and that will go lower still—for these three reasons:

## 1. The Game of Politics

With both major political parties vying to show which one is more fiscally responsible, ever-increasing government spending is not likely. While the 1984 presidential campaign is otherwise eminently forgettable, it offered the interesting spectacle of a liberal Democrat attacking a conservative Republican for failure to cut government spending. Slowly, erratically, imperfectly, the government is likely to check its free-spending ways.

## 2. The Social Security Kicker

Still, you might object, the resolve of politicians tends to go the way of ice cream in the sun. And even if it is true that a relatively high debt ratio can coexist with a long-term bull market, at some point the debt ratio could get too high, triggering an inflationary spiral.

Again this is true—in theory. But for a reason that just about no one has fully grasped, there is virtually no chance that the debt ratio will rise over the next thirty-five to fifty years—in fact, it is almost guaranteed to decline. The reason is a monumental *overfunding* of Social Security.

When President Reagan took office in 1981, one of the most pressing problems facing the country was the potential bankruptcy of the Social Security system. A bipartisan committee was formed to produce a solution. Headed by respected economist Alan Greenspan, it came up with a plan that in 1983 was approved by Congress virtually intact. Everybody congratulated himself on a job well done.

In fact, it was a job *too* well done. The tax increases enacted by Congress promise to overfund the system by a staggering extent for the next thirty-five to fifty years. And this has a direct impact on the debt ratio.

Essentially, the overfunding came about because of psychology and what is invariably referred to as the magic of compounding. When the Greenspan commission was deliberating, the economy was in the midst of a severe recession. No one was forecasting strong future growth. This is relevant because the taxes needed to fund Social Security are intimately tied to future economic growth. The greater the growth, the larger the tax base on which to draw.

Moreover, the commission was trying to design a plan that could meet the needs of retirees seventy-five or more years out. The problem is that long-term planning based on a psychologically short-term perspective can lead to some very strange results.

The reason is the magic of compounding. Com-

49

pounding has the effect over time of magnifying small miscalculations, turning them into very large miscalculations. Over time, the commission's overly pessimistic assumptions about future economic growth will result in a huge buildup of funds in the Social Security system.

Stuart J. Sweet, a legislative assistant to Senator Paula Hawkins, Republican of Florida, has studied the likely effects of the 1983 Social Security funding amendments. *He concludes that the system will build a surplus of more than $1 trillion in real dollars over the next fifteen years.* Others believe the surplus will be even greater. By the middle of the next century the surplus could be $20 trillion or more.

But this is only half the story. Let me quote from an editorial in *The Wall Street Journal* of February 11, 1985. Referring to the projected surplus, it says: "The interesting quirk in all this is that the trust fund's debt impact is not reflected in federal deficit numbers. Those deficits . . . out into the future . . . do not at all reflect what amounts to a steady and countervailing retirement of federal debt. That's because payments into the trust fund are treated as a federal 'expenditure' even though they are going into portfolio investment."

The implications of this latter statement are extraordinary. Not only will future budget deficits almost surely be covered by Social Security surpluses. But figured into the deficit is something that actually should be considered as surplus—payments into the Social Security system. To project "real" future deficits, the Social Security surplus, therefore, should be subtracted *twice.* The upshot is that under current actuarial and economic assumptions, by 1989 the cumulative surplus will reduce the projected budget deficit to about 0. In effect, the deficit will vanish—even if the government does nothing, in the form of tax increases or spending cuts, to reduce it.

Here are two predictions. Sometime within the next five years, the current deficit fear is going to be replaced with a fear of surplus. After all, investing *trillions* of dollars is no easy matter. Relatedly, Reagan, the great tax-cutter, is almost a sure bet to go down in history as Reagan, the great tax-hiker, as the surplus results from much higher than needed taxes to fund the Social Security system.

## 3. The Paul to Peter to Paul Principle

I hope you're convinced by now that the deficit is an empty issue. But there's more. Suppose for a moment that everything I've said so far is wrong. The deficit still would be irrelevant. This is because of something that I call the Paul to Peter to Paul principle.

Early in 1985 Martin Feldstein, former chairman of the Council of Economic Advisers, argued that the biggest problem with the deficit is interest payments. Remember, deficits add to total debt. Increased debt means greater interest payments, these in turn add to total debt, and so on. Or so it seemed to Feldstein.

The Paul to Peter to Paul principle explains why Feldstein's fears are unfounded. For it shows why the interest payment portion of the deficit, far from being a burden remediable only by tax increases, actually sharply *reduces* the burden of the deficit.

An example will show you why. Suppose you have a

51

friend who constantly borrows money from you. Your name is Paul, his name is Peter. At the end of ten years Peter owes you $10,000. Friendship has its limits, and you decide to start charging Peter interest of 10% a year. The following year Peter borrows no additional money. But you want him to start paying back some of what he owes. You ask him for $1000, one year's interest payment. Guess what? Peter, not having the $1000, has to borrow it, and he turns to you. What can you do? You hand him the $1000, which he dutifully returns to you as an interest payment. The money has gone from Paul to Peter to Paul.

The situation with government interest payments is a little more complicated, but the basic principle is the same. As Peter Bernstein, a well-regarded economist, noted in *The Wall Street Journal* on January 8, 1985, "the interest payments made by the government do not go up in smoke. . . . They either add to savings streams directly or they accrue indirectly to people who make use of various types of savings institutions." In other words, from Paul to Peter to Paul.

Let's summarize why the deficit isn't the problem most people assume it is.

First, it's the debt ratio, not the deficit ratio, that counts most in terms of rising inflation. The debt ratio today is not particularly high by historical standards, nor is it likely to go higher. One reason is that under the current political climate the deficit, while still measuring in the billions, is almost certain to be trimmed. And even a constant-sized deficit would result in a declining debt ratio.

Second, enormous Social Security surpluses will neutralize the deficit, further assurance that the debt ratio will actually decline, as it did during both secular bull markets of the past.

Third, even if everything I've said so far is wrong, the deficit still wouldn't matter because the interest payment portion of it—which is what everyone is most concerned about—under the Paul to Peter to Paul principle goes directly into the savings stream.

The deficit, that bogeyman of the 1980s, is a phony issue. It poses no threat to sustained economic growth—or to the secular bull.

# 3

# WHEN GROWTH IS KING

***Condition No. 1:*** *Real growth must be greater than inflation.*

You should now better understand the relationship between growth and stocks and between sustained growth and secular bull markets. And it should be clearer why, if you can develop accurate ways of forecasting sustainable growth, you have at the same time discovered how to forecast a secular bull market.

This brings us back to my first condition for predicting both sustainable growth and a secular bull market. It is: *Real growth must be greater than inflation.*

As you probably remember from Economics 1, growth—known as nominal growth—has two components, real growth and inflation. Real growth is unit growth. In terms of an individual company, it means making and selling more products, winning over new customers. In terms of the economy as a whole, it means that total output rises. Real growth is just what it says: It is real. It is honest.

Companies can also grow by raising prices. If a company sells 1000 radios one year and 1000 the next, but the first year it charges $20 per radio and the second year $25, it will show a growth rate of 25%. It hasn't increased its actual output a whit, but through the magic of inflation it is showing great growth. When inflation is general, the economy may look as if it is growing rapidly, but growth that comes solely from inflation is an illusion. More houses aren't being built and furnished, more goods aren't being sold, no one is benefiting from such growth.

When the real component of growth is greater than the illusory component, growth can continue. When the illusory component is greater, growth is doomed.

The fact that inflation is what plays the spoiler role in the economy is, by itself, no great revelation to anyone who lived through the boom-bust years of the late 1960s and 1970s. Throughout that time, as every economic recovery progressed, inflation would inexorably start to gain momentum. The economy would overheat, and a recession would be the upshot. Because of accelerating inflation, growth was never sustained for very long, and neither were rising stock prices.

Uncontrolled inflation is a social and economic evil. However, a little inflation isn't so terrible. If prices are rising by, say, 2% a year, that is something that in all likelihood businesses and consumers can live with. Businesses can still make rational investment decisions about building new plants and expanding into new markets by simply taking into account a 2% rise in prices. Individuals will still find it worthwhile to save for the future. This is the crux: When inflation remains relatively low and predictable, businesses and individuals can behave as if there *is* a future. Thus, a certain degree of inflation is not automatically incompatible with sustained growth.

Inflation becomes a threat to growth when it keeps accelerating—ending in runaway inflation—for two reasons. First, as I've suggested, as inflation accelerates, no one bothers with the long-term planning that would ensure real future growth. It is impossible for either businesses or consumers to behave as if there were a future over which they had any control. Instead of investing in new plant and equipment—which would lay the groundwork for real growth for years to come—businesses give in to the temptation to grow the easy way, by raising prices. Consumers, too, become unwilling to save; they figure they might as well spend, spend, spend, today, for tomorrow everything will cost more. Everyone focuses on the shorter term, and the longer term gets lost. The result has, historically, been a breakdown of the economy.

Second, because the dangers of runaway inflation are so great, as inflation gathers momentum it is a sure bet that the Federal Reserve will take action to quell it, such as tightening up on the money supply. The worse the inflation, the more Draconian the response. Such action invariably tamps down inflation at the cost of bringing on a recession, the antithesis of growth. Either way, growth is sure to be short-circuited.

So some inflation is tolerable, but a little more may be too much. No one, however, has ever really pinpointed how much is too much. If inflation is at 3%, is that too high? Should the Federal Reserve tighten the screws? If it climbs to 4%, is economic growth doomed and should investors buy gold and run for the hills? The question of how much inflation is too much has occupied the Fed, Congress, economists, and many laymen, but no one has determined the crucial moment at which a docile, well-behaved inflation becomes the monster runaway inflation.

The reason is that everyone has focused on the wrong thing. They have tried to pinpoint a specific level of inflation—4%, 5%, etc.—when in fact the answer revolves around the *relative* rather than the *absolute* value of inflation. It is a question of a *relationship*—the relationship between inflation and real growth. It is like a man on a diving board ten feet above the pool who wants to know if it is safe to jump. If all he knows is the height of the board, it's just so much guesswork. You have to know the depth of the water, too.

My first condition specifies the level at which inflation becomes a danger in terms of how it stacks up against real growth. It says that it doesn't matter if inflation is at 4%, 6%, or higher, *as long as it remains below real growth*. When real growth is greater than inflation, inflation will remain well behaved and growth is sustainable. When inflation overtakes real growth, that is when inflation turns into runaway inflation, overheating the economy and making it head into a recession.

In the early 1950s, for example, inflation was much higher than in the early 1930s, but in the 1950s it remained below real growth. And the market made strong gains in the 1950s, whereas it showed a steady decline in the early 1930s.

I determined this first and most basic condition for a secular bull market by looking at the relationship between inflation and real growth, going back as far as

1890, and tracking this relationship against both economic growth levels and the stock market. For convenience's sake, I expressed the condition as a ratio, the ratio of real growth to inflation. It is easy to see that, if this ratio is above 1, it is exactly the same as saying that real growth is greater than inflation. (If real growth is 5% and inflation 4%, the ratio is above 1. If, however, inflation at 5% is greater than real growth at, say, 3%, the ratio will be below 1.) Thus, another way to say that this condition has been fulfilled is to say that the ratio between real growth and inflation is greater than 1.*

Real growth refers to real growth in the Gross National Product. For my measure of inflation I used the broadest possible yardstick, the GNP Price Deflator. This measures prices across the board rather than some presumed typical market basket of goods, as is measured by the better-known Consumer Price Index.

Figure 3-1 tells much of the story. What it shows is that over a span of more than ninety years, when the ratio was above 1, the stock market, as measured by the S&P 400, rose on average 10.54% the following year. When the ratio fell below 1, the market declined an average of 3.80%. The higher the ratio—meaning the more that real growth exceeded inflation—the greater the gains in the market.

Because I thought it possible that the two major wars that occurred during this period might have skewed the

---

*The statistically minded should please note that to keep the ratio consistently defined regardless of whether growth was negative or positive, I added a large constant—I arbitrarily chose 100—to both terms, inflation and real growth. Thus, if real growth were 5% and inflation 3%, the ratio would actually be 105:103 instead of 5:3, still above 1. That way, if real growth were negative at −5% and prices were falling by 3%, the ratio, instead of being −5:−3, which would be an erroneous positive signal, would be 95:103, below 1 and a correct negative signal.

58

results, I repeated the study, leaving out those years. As you can see in Figure 3-1, the results still bear out the thesis: When the ratio was above 1, the market rose 9.83%, whereas it showed a decline of 0.34% when the ratio was below 1.

**FIGURE 3-1**

## THE RATIO AND MARKET GAINS

| | **Average Change in S&P 400** | |
| | *Excluding* | *Including* |
| Ratio | WWs | WWs |
| --- | --- | --- |
| 1.06 to 1.22 | 14.42% | 13.92% |
| 1.02 to 1.05 | 11.47 | 10.24 |
| 1.01 to 1.00 | 6.61 | 5.02 |
| 0.99 to 0.96 | 4.12 | 3.94 |
| Less than 0.96 | −8.76 | −5.12 |
| | | |
| 1.00 or more | 10.54% | 9.83% |
| Less than 1.0 | −3.80% | −0.34% |

These numbers may seem dry, but they are enormously significant, for they tell you that the relationship I have presented to you, real growth greater than inflation, isn't just mumbo jumbo: It has a direct bearing on what the stock market does—it has predictive value, which is all that you can ask of any stock market indicator. When the condition is in place, the market advances strongly. When it is not, the market declines.

And there is even more to it than that. As you can see from Figure 3-2, the ratio also predicts growth in the

Gross National Product. When the ratio is high, not only do stock prices rise, but GNP growth the following year tends to be high. When the ratio is low, GNP growth the following year tends to be low. When the ratio is greater than 1, GNP growth the following year is on average more than twice what it is when the ratio is below 1. In other words, my study has also confirmed my original premise that stock market gains are related to sustainable growth, and that growth is sustainable when inflation is below real growth. When the ratio was above 1, growth was strong the next year—i.e., growth proved sustainable—and at the same time the market advanced.

## FIGURE 3-2

## THE RATIO AND GNP GROWTH

| Ratio | GNP Growth One Year Later |
|---|---|
| 1.06 to 1.22 | 5.22% |
| 1.05 to 1.02 | 4.35 |
| 1.01 to 1.00 | 3.49 |
| 0.96 to 0.99 | 2.82 |
| Less than 0.96 | 0.95 |
| 1.00 or greater | 4.39% |
| Less than 1.00 | 1.94% |

This study provides strong evidence that my first condition works. But by necessity the study was formulated in terms of average market gains and losses. How, specifically, would my ratio have helped you perform in the secular bull markets of the past? Exceedingly well, as I'll show you.

First, let's review the signals from my ratio, starting with the secular bull market of the 1920s. In the five years prior to 1921, the average growth rate was only 2.5%, while inflation was a staggering 13.77%. The ratio, clearly, was saying that the economy was not close to entering a period of sustained growth. But in 1921 a fundamental change took place. The economy, plagued by excess capacity, slumped into a postwar recession. That brief period of pain brought inflation down from the stratosphere, and in 1921 prices declined by nearly 15%. Real growth also turned negative, though at −8.7% it was above the inflation rate for the first time since 1912–1913. The ratio, in other words, had moved above 1 in the context of negative growth.

In 1922, however, not only was the ratio above 1 but, with real growth an extremely healthy 15.8% and inflation still declining, it was above 1 in the context of positive economic growth. And real growth continued to be greater than inflation throughout the 1920s. From 1921 to 1929 real growth averaged 4.5% while inflation was just a shade greater than −2%.

The post–World War II market had a similar beginning. Starting in 1945, inflation began to exceed real growth. In the four years before the war, inflation averaged 8% while real growth averaged a depressing −2.5%, except for the early 1930s the worst four-year period in this century. Despite the economy's poor performance, inflation had to be crushed, and starting in 1947 the Federal Reserve, wittingly or not, began to contract the money supply. As a result, the economy, which had begun to recover in 1948, turned down again in 1949, with real growth just about nil for the year. But inflation in 1949 dropped all the way down into negative territory. My ratio had once again fallen into place and the market was once again off to the races.

The behavior of inflation during the 1949–1965 period, though not as extraordinary as in the 1920s, was still exceptional, averaging just a shade over 2%. Real growth averaged 4.1%, more than twice as high, and keeping my ratio, on average, above 1 for the entire period.

But the averages conceal a few bumps and jolts, and during this sixteen-year stretch there were four years— 1954, 1956, 1957, and 1958—in which inflation exceeded real growth. The first, 1954, was a recession year in which real growth was negative at −1.4%. But that was no real problem: As you will see later, Condition No. 4, growth in the money supply, would have assured you that the recession posed no long-term threat to the bull market.

The years 1956–1958 are a different story, however, and this period is probably best viewed as a pause in the secular bull market. In both 1956 and 1957 growth was positive but, at an average rate of 1.6%, clearly on the low side. Slow but positive growth is fine as long as inflation advances even more slowly. In 1961 real growth was less than 2% but inflation was even lower, and the market as measured by the S&P 400 scored a stunning 17.8% advance. But in 1956 inflation was 3.4% and it rose to 3.7% in 1957. The Fed responded by tightening the monetary screws, and what followed was nine months of the worst recession in the post–World War II period. (While the 1953–1954 recession lasted longer, the contraction in economic activity was less severe.)

As 1958 progressed, it was clear that the recession had cleared the air. Economic growth resumed—and at a rate greater than inflation. My ratio swung back into place just as the second phase of the secular bull market was starting. And the ratio remained in place through 1965.

The years that followed 1965 gave rise to a new economic phenomenon, the boom-bust cycles that have come to seem as inevitable as polluted air to the last few generations of investors. Actually, at least part of the term is a misnomer in that the so-called booms would have been characterized as mere ordinary economic growth had they occurred in the 1920s or in the 1949–1965 period. The busts were something else again. In fairly rapid succession the period from 1966 to 1982 produced three major recessions that, especially the last two, were unlike anything that had been seen in the recent past. Between the second quarter of 1969 and the last quarter of 1970 the economy averaged no net real growth. Not since after the end of World War II had economic growth been stagnant for so long.

There was worse to come. After a recovery that spanned 1971–1973, the economy went into another tailspin and for the next two consecutive years, 1974 and 1975, registered negative economic growth. Recovery followed, only to be short-circuited by the worst recession since the Depression. The years 1980, 1981, and 1982 saw only one quarter of solid economic growth in three years.

Was the ratio below 1 throughout this period, as you would expect? Yes. Inflation averaged 6% and real growth just a shade above 2½%. In only two years, 1968 and 1972, was inflation below real growth. But during those years there also was clear evidence from my other conditions that these positive developments would be ephemeral, as in fact they turned out to be.

What about my ratio in the mini secular bull market of 1933–1937? Then, too, it remained decidedly above 1. For the years 1933 through 1936, real growth in GNP averaged 7½%, while inflation as measured by the GNP Price Deflator averaged only a shade above 1½%, despite a flareup in agricultural prices in 1934. Only in 1937, as the market was turning down, did the ratio move back below 1.

Thus, whether you're looking at the average figures, as in the study of my ratio, or at specific market periods, my first condition has great predictive value. The ratio correlates highly with sustained economic growth and secular bull markets. Any investor who did nothing but follow my ratio would have been in the market during the bulk of each secular bull market and out of it at virtually all other times.

However, good as it is, it cannot stand alone. There can be transitory dips or spurts in both growth and inflation that occasionally result in misleading signals. Moreover, because of lags in reporting data on real growth and inflation, my ratio can be a little late at turning points. One example is 1929, when broad-based reported data on the economy still showed a positive ratio even when it was clear by other measures that the economy had finally turned sour. This is why in addition to the ratio we also need my remaining three conditions. These three serve as lead indicators to the first, and most basic, condition. They help let you know if the ratio is about to rise above 1 and also, in certain cases, if a ratio above or below 1 is a false signal.

Two questions may have occurred to you:

First, why have economists, with all their complex econometric models, failed to discover the key importance of the relationship between real growth and inflation in predicting sustainable growth? There may be many reasons for this, but the most important is the tendency of economists to think in *linear terms*.

To explain what I mean, let's switch to the laboratory of one Dr. Edward Lorenz, a researcher at the Massachusetts Institute of Technology in the 1960s. Lorenz, a mathematician, was studying weather patterns. He made an interesting discovery: that extremely minute changes in one atmospheric variable, such as temperature, in one place could have a dramatic effect on weather conditions elsewhere. For example, if the temperature in Chicago at a particular hour were 74.111234˙ degrees, New York might enjoy balmy weather a few days later. If, instead, the Chicago reading were 74.111233 degrees, New Yorkers might be in for a violent thunderstorm. Or, as it has been more poetically expressed, the beating of a butterfly's wings in Hong Kong can affect the weather in London a month later.

The mathematical term for this kind of relationship, in which a very small change has a very big impact, is *nonlinear* relationship. Such relationships are common in mathematics, science, the social sciences, and everyday life. To give one homely example, sprinkling your steak with a tiny amount of sugar instead of salt is a very small change that would have an enormous impact on how much you enjoyed your dinner.

If you look at how the typical economic forecast is derived, you will see that economists tend to think strictly in linear terms. They assume, for example, that a small change in inflation will have a correspondingly small impact on interest rates when, in fact, the impact may be quite large. Linear relationships are far simpler to work with, and they do perform fairly well much of the time, which is why economists continue to rely on them. However, they break down at major economic turning points—such as the shift from a cyclical economy to one characterized by secular growth.

My first condition is an example of a nonlinear relationship. Inherent in it is the notion that a seemingly small change in inflation may mean the difference between recession and a secular bull market. If real growth is 4% and inflation is 3½%, my ratio is above 1, growth is sustainable, and a secular bull market is highly probable. If inflation rises just one point, to 4½%, the ratio falls below 1, growth is not sustainable, and the secular bull market goes out the window. Since economists don't think in nonlinear terms, it isn't surprising that they haven't discovered this ratio.

The second question is, Why is it just at the point where inflation passes real growth that inflation turns into hyperinflation and growth becomes unsustainable? My study of the ratio since 1890 proves that this is so, and intuitively it seems to make sense, but I do not have a mathematical or theoretical reason for it. So instead of trying to give an explanation, I will end this chapter with a little fable, which may serve just as well.

Let's imagine a high school biology class with thirty students. When the school year opens, all of them, bright and idealistic, are eager to study hard and learn, and they assume that hard work is the path to good grades. When exam time comes around they are willing to crack the books, for that is the only way they know to do well. This studying is the equivalent of real growth.

Now let's suppose that one student, we'll call him Tony, has gone to a movie the night before an exam instead of studying. He gets into class, looks at the exam in front of him, and realizes that he doesn't know any of the answers. Then it occurs to him that if he can just sneak a look at the paper of the student next to him, Andrea, he may come out all right. He does, and he gets an A. Tony has accumulated another good grade—but this time there has been no growth in his real knowledge.

So far this cheating isn't a major problem, since everyone but Tony is still studying hard. But now suppose that a third student, Robert, finds out how Tony really got that A in biology. Robert isn't really that interested in amoebas and asexual reproduction, and when the next exam time rolls around he deliberately goes out on a date the night before the biology test. That morning he carefully sits down next to Bruce, a straight-A student. Robert passes with flying colors, as does Tony, who once again has grabbed a seat next to Andrea.

Like an infection, the cheating spreads. As more students realize that they can get good grades without studying, the remaining students start to figure that

67

they must be saps for working so hard when they are not being any better rewarded than those who don't work at all. When just a few students are cheating, the disease is containable. When too many students are cheating, everyone throws in the towel and concentrates on short-term grades rather than on long-term learning. Drastic action may be necessary, such as expelling half the class.

This is just an analogy, of course, not an explanation. But I like it because I tend to think of inflation as a form of cheating, and I would prefer to see companies rewarded for hard work in producing better products at a lower cost rather than for raising prices. I don't like to see real growth, or real knowledge, cheapened by false counterparts.

# 4

# BOND YIELDS: THE REAL STORY

*Condition No. 2: Bond yields must be twice the inflation rate—"real real rates" must be positive.*

Investors in stocks today care passionately about the course of interest rates. And it is an article of faith that when rates go up, stocks come down. That assumption seems as logical and self-evident as asserting that a January freeze is bad for Florida's citrus growers.

The reasoning is simple: As rates rise, investors become increasingly likely to withdraw their money from the stock market and put it into safer, high-yielding, fixed-income instruments. As cash flows out of the market, stock prices drop. At the same time, higher rates, by making it more expensive for businesses to borrow money, choke off economic growth. Unable to afford the money they need to continue operations or to expand, existing businesses contract or fail altogether, while new businesses can't get off the ground. Unemployment goes up, and the economy enters another bust phase.

Like one domino crashing into the next, until the whole row has fallen, rising rates set off a chain of events leading inevitably to recession and a bear market.

Or so investors of the early 1980s have been conditioned to believe. And they have been aided and abetted in this belief by the great majority of market analysts—people who should know better. In fact, almost from the moment this bull market began in August 1982 I have been hearing that historically high interest rates would rule out a major bull move. Even as stocks continued their ascent, analysts continued to argue that rates—and in particular the high level of long-term-rates—posed an imminent threat to the bull.

*But virtually everyone has missed the real point about the relationship between interest rates and stocks—which is that under the right circumstances high and rising rates are entirely compatible with a sustained bull market.*

Note that I say "under the right circumstances." During the cyclical, inflation-ridden late 1960s and 1970s, circumstances were emphatically not right, and rising rates did go hand in hand with a contracting economy and falling stocks.

In December 1968, for example, long-term rates, as measured by S&P-rated AAA bonds, were at 6.4%. The S&P 400 averaged 116 for the month, then an all-time high. Throughout 1969, however, rates rose. By mid-1970, bonds were at 8.2%. This turned out to be the peak. But meanwhile the market had been relentlessly sinking. By the time bonds hit their highs, the S&P 400 was near 80.

As rates began to drop, the market embarked upon a major rally. By early 1971 bonds had dropped to 7.15%, and soon the S&P 400 had recovered almost all its lost ground and was trading near 115. But not for long. Rates once again began to climb, and the market plummeted anew.

Let's move ahead a little. In January 1973, the S&P 400 averaged 132.60, a record high for the time. Bonds were at 7.3%. Throughout the year, long-term rates rose, eventually hitting 7.7%. As rates climbed, a major bear market developed. By the end of the year the S&P 400 had fallen some 20%, to 106.20, while the secondary stocks had come down even more sharply. And this was just the start. As bond rates continued to edge up— to an ultimate high of nearly 9%—the market, after rallying briefly in the early part of 1974, resumed its downward slide. By the end of September 1974, the S&P 400 was at 69.53.

But relief was in sight. Most long-term rates peaked just as the market was bottoming in the fall of 1974. The decline in rates continued with few interruptions all the way through the powerful 1975–1976 bull market. By the end of 1976, long-time yields had fallen below 8% for the first time in more than two and a half years, and the S&P 400 was averaging 116.30.

And so on and so forth. From the mid-1960s on, the correlation between rising rates and falling stocks was extremely strong. It was like a seesaw: When one end goes up, the other goes down.

But a longer-term perspective—one that encompasses the secular bull markets of the 1920s and the 1949–1965 era—shows that *rising rates can also go hand in hand with rising stock prices.* In those years, instead of a seesaw, what you had was something akin to a nauseating ride I remember from the days when the Palisades Park amusement park was still flourishing, a whirligig in which everybody was spun up into the air at the same time.

Look at what happened in the mid-1950s, for example. In January 1955, the S&P 400 averaged 36.8, and bonds were yielding 2.9%. By April 1956, bonds had climbed to 3.2%—and the S&P 400 had risen almost 40%, to 51.38.

In December 1960 bonds were yielding 4.37% and the S&P 400 was at 60.22. A year later bonds were yielding 4.42%. The S&P 400? The rise in rates hadn't bothered it at all: It was sitting at a lofty 75.81.

Some more evidence: In October 1962, following the major correction that had sent the market skidding throughout much of that year, the S&P 400 was at 58.66 and bond rates were 4.20%. A year later bonds were up to 4.30%—while the S&P 400 had rallied to 77.09.

Finally, returning to the first great secular bull market, it is true that bond yields declined slightly, from 5.1% to 4.5%, between 1922 and 1929. But this modest drop was in no way commensurate with the more than fivefold gain in stock prices during that period. Moreover, because prices were also dropping, rates rose in real terms.

Rising rates, then, are apparently deadly for the market some of the time and as inconsequential as a summer breeze at other times. On the surface it is all very confusing, and you might understandably be tempted to conclude that perhaps interest rates don't count at all when it comes to predicting what stocks will do.

But rates do count, very much. And they count for the very same reason that most people think they do:

72

because they give you a clue about the prospects for economic growth. It's just that the relationship between rates and growth is not as simplistic as most investors—both amateurs and pros—think.

To explain exactly what I mean, let's start by getting back to the basics—by looking at exactly what interest rates are.

## 1. Expectations of Growth

Interest rates are, obviously, the amount that you can earn on any money that you put in, say, a savings account or a certificate of deposit. They are also what you must pay on money that you borrow to buy a house or a car, or what businesses must pay to borrow funds to finance a new factory or to purchase new equipment.

But what determines whether your money earns 5% instead of 7%? And why is it that, for a business to borrow $100,000, one year it might have to pay 6% and another year only 4%? Why does money cost more at some times than at others?

Forget for now everything you have ever heard about the Fed and raising and lowering the discount rate and all other such arcane matters that bear on interest rates. *At the most basic level, what determines the level of interest rates is that old Adam Smith standby, supply and demand.* When demand for money rises, or is expected to rise, the cost of money goes up. When demand falls, or is expected to fall, the cost goes down.

Here is where growth comes in. Demand—or the lack of it—is intimately related to expectations of growth. When businesses are confidently expecting to grow, it is worth their while to borrow money to finance this growth. Demand for money will increase, and therefore so will the cost of money—i.e., interest rates will rise. The more growth businesses expect, the more they will be willing to pay for the money they need. Conversely, when businesses are not expecting to grow, the demand for money will drop, and interest rates will come down.

*Interest rates reflect the expectations of a lot of businesses about growth.* And in particular, *long-term rates reflect expectations about growth.* Short-term rates, such as Fed funds and T-bills, show mostly what is happening in the present. Long-term rates, by contrast, are future-oriented. They show what businesses expect their needs for money will be over the next several years. If a corporation is willing to issue a twenty-year bond paying 10% a year, it implies that the company is expecting to invest the money it receives in enterprises that will result in earnings growth of better than 10% a year over those twenty years. Otherwise it wouldn't make sense to issue the bond in the first place. (It's not quite as simple as all that. Tax considerations, for example, also play a role in the taking on of debt and affect the numbers involved. But the basic principle holds.)

If all this sounds a little too neat to be true, consider the following. From 1922 through 1985, long-term rates, as measured by AAA bonds, have averaged 5.2%. During the same period, the growth rate of earnings for the companies that make up the Dow Jones Industrial Average has also averaged 5.2%, while GNP growth has averaged about 5.8%.

The closeness of these numbers is no coincidence.

The point is that, admittedly with erratic lags, long-term rates have been a good proxy for long-term economic growth. This is strong confirmation of the notion that interest rates do reflect expectations about growth. Moreover, the fact that rates have correlated so closely over time with actual growth shows that the expectations are firmly rooted in reality.

## 2. Real versus Nominal Rates

There is a second fact about rates that you must grasp, and the concept will be familiar to you: the notion of *real* rates as opposed to *nominal* rates. This is the same distinction as that between real growth and nominal growth. Real rates are nominal rates minus inflation. In the case of interest rates, nominal rates are the actual number at which rates are pegged.

For example, if you pass a bank that has a notice in its window that it is offering 10% interest on a 12-month certificate of deposit, that 10% is the nominal rate. If, tempted by the window display, you go into the bank and put $1000 into a certificate of deposit, then, at the end of the year, forgetting about compounding, you will have $1100. But if inflation has also been running at 10%, when you take your money out at the end of the year, your $1100 will buy you no more than you could have gotten at the beginning of the year with your $1000. So in effect you haven't earned anything. The real rate of interest you have earned is 10% minus 10%, or zero. If, however, inflation is 4%, then of the $100 extra in your pocket $40 goes to inflation and $60 represents actual new buying power. In this case real rates are 6%.

## 3. Real Rates = Real Growth

Real rates reflect expectations about real growth. If you think about it, this will seem obvious. Suppose that nominal interest rates are 12%. This means that businesses are expecting to grow by 12%. But if inflation is 5%, then 5 of those 12 percentage points will come from price increases. Only the remaining 7 percentage points of growth are expected to come through real growth, unit growth.

We can now see the significance of my second condition: Growth is sustainable, and secular bull markets possible, only when long-term interest rates (bond yields) are more than twice the inflation rate.

If you think back to the first condition—real growth that is greater than inflation—it will become clear why the second condition must also hold. *For only when interest rates are more than twice inflation is it true that the expectations are for real growth that is greater than inflation.* If interest rates are 12%, for example, and inflation is less than half of that—say, 4%—then real rates (a proxy for real growth) are 8%—greater than inflation and therefore no bar to sustainable growth. If, instead, inflation rises to above half of 12%—say, to 7%—then real rates are only 5%, less than inflation and therefore a warning that growth will not prove sustainable.

So we have come around again, through the path of interest rates, to the underlying condition for a secular bull market: real growth that is greater than inflation. Given the relationship between interest rates and growth, Condition No. 2 is the inevitable counterpart to Condition No. 1.

Now you can understand why, despite what most people assume, high and rising rates can happily coexist with a soaring stock market. Only when the inflationary component of interest rates is greater than the real component, as was largely the case during the cyclical economies of the 1966–1982 period, are rising rates negative for stocks. In those years, rising rates generally reflected inflation that was overwhelming real growth. By contrast, during the 1920s and the 1950s and early 1960s rising rates simply meant that businesses were expecting substantial real growth. That is why, in those years, rising rates didn't deter the stock market at all.

But here you may ask, if the second condition for sustainable growth and a long-term bull market is derived from the first, why do we need it? Why not just concentrate on the first condition? Why confuse things by bringing in interest rates at all?

For one thing, you simply can't ignore interest rates. Like Mount Everest, they are there, and any theory that attempts to give a comprehensive explanation of the interplay between the economy and the stock market must take interest rates into account. By understanding how rising rates can be positively related to economic growth, you will have a more complete understanding of growth itself.

But more generally, it is important to reiterate that no single one of my four conditions is a magic, infallible indicator that stands entirely on its own. Rather, each gives you a slightly different perspective on whether or not growth is sustainable. You have to weigh all of them together. Furthermore, the other conditions can serve as lead indicators to the first condition.

Take 1949, for example. Early in the year, as inflation dropped, interest rates for the first time in a while were more than twice the inflation rate: Condition No. 2 was flashing a buy signal. But the ratio of real growth to inflation didn't move above 1 until later in the year. If you had gone by just the ratio, you would have missed the first part of the big bull rally that began that year. But with the advance warning from the second condition (as well as from the fourth, as you'll see later), you could have been confident that the ratio was destined to turn bullish, and you would have gotten in the market by the spring, just as the second secular bull market was starting.

Similarly, a negative signal from the second condition can tell you to get out of the market even though the growth ratio is still in place. This was the case in 1937, for instance. In January of that year the second condition turned bearish with the Dow in the 180s. If you had just been following the ratio, however, you would have stayed in the market a good while longer, and this would have been a bad mistake: The ratio remained bullish until the end of the year, by which time the Dow was in the 120s.

Condition No. 1 is essential to a secular bull market. Its existence is at the very heart of a long-term bull market; it is what gives such a market life. But Condition No. 2 (and the other two) must also exist for us to have confidence that the first condition can remain in place, and these other conditions can also let you know in advance that the first condition will soon be moving into place. The conditions work as a team, and they all are necessary for the secular bull.

## "Real Real Rates": A First-Rate Indicator

Condition No. 2, then, works hand in glove with the ratio of real growth to inflation and with the remaining two conditions to predict secular bull markets. But it turns out that if you look at Condition No. 2 alone you also have an exceptional indicator, even apart from the major secular bull markets—an indicator with a superb record of catching shorter-term bull and bear shifts.

Another way of expressing my second condition is in terms of "real real rates." These are defined as the difference between real interest rates (nominal rates less inflation) and inflation. For example, if real interest rates are 6% and inflation is 4%, real real rates are 2%. If, however, real rates are 6% but inflation is 8%, real real rates are $-2\%$. It is easy to see that when real real rates are positive, it means that the expectations are for real growth that is greater than inflation (sustainable growth). When real real rates are negative, the expectations are for real growth that is less than inflation (growth that is not sustainable).

I have done a detailed study of real real rates covering the past thirty years. As the measure of inflation I used the twelve-month rate of change in the Producer Price Index, a lead indicator of consumer inflation. For my measure of interest rates I used AAA bond yields. (To smooth things out I used a five-month average of real real rates, though the results would have been similar had I used an average of anywhere from one to twelve months.) When the five-month average of real real rates was positive, it was a buy signal. When the average turned negative, it was a sell signal.

Figure 4-1 shows the exceedingly accurate results. In thirty years the indicator has given just ten signals. Nine of them were correct: When real real rates turned positive, the market gained significantly over the long term. Between June 1956 and May 1985 real real rates were positive for a total of a little more than sixteen years, during which time the S&P 400 gained nearly 500%. Before dividends, this works out to an an-

**FIGURE 4-1**

## SIGNALS FROM REAL REAL RATES INDICATOR

| Date | Indicator | S&P 400 | % Change To Next Signal |
|------|-----------|---------|-------------------------|
| 6/56 | Bearish | 49.38 | − 12.3 |
| 12/57 | Bullish | 43.29 | + 119.3 |
| 9/65 | Bearish | 94.43 | − 8.9 |
| 1/67 | Bullish | 86.50 | + 19.9 |
| 7/69 | Bearish | 103.70 | − 19.9 |
| 6/70 | Bullish | 83.16 | + 49.6 |
| 9/72 | Bearish | 124.40 | − 8.4 |
| 10/76 | Bullish | 114.00 | + 1.1 |
| 1/77 | Bearish | 115.20 | + 18.8 |
| 11/81 | Bullish | 136.80 | + 47.8 |
| May 1985 | | 202.13 | |

nualized gain of 11.5%. When real rates turned negative, the market dropped. Only one signal, in effect from 1977 to 1981, could be considered wrong in that it was bearish while the market gained 18.8%. But during that period the market underperformed nearly all other possible investments, including T-bills and most tangible assets, and thus represented an opportunity cost.

Real real rates gave a buy signal in late 1981. Since then the S&P 400 has gained more than 47%. With the buy signal still in effect, the very strong message from the second condition—as from the first—is that the bull is in no danger of flagging any time soon.

# 5

# INTEREST RATES, SHORT AND LONG

*Condition No. 3:* *Short-term interest rates must be lower than long-term rates.*

My third condition—short-term interest rates that are below long-term rates—is a bit different from the preceding two in that it was in place during most of the first half of the century, during bull and bear, cyclical and secular, markets alike. So obviously if you see that short-term rates are lower than long-term rates, it doesn't necessarily mean that it is time to buy stocks. The converse, however, is true: If long-term rates fall below short-term rates—or if the spread between them narrows significantly—you know it is time to pull out of stocks or at least to become exceedingly cautious.

Why is it curtains for the market when short-term rates surpass long-term rates? As always, it comes back to a question of sustainable growth. I have emphasized that *long-term rates* reflect expectations of growth—real growth plus inflation. That is because rates reflect the demand for money, and businesses are not willing to pay to borrow money unless they believe that they will be growing fast enough to justify the cost.

By contrast, *short-term rates* tend to reflect inflationary expectations more than expectations of real growth. The shorter the maturity, the greater the role you can surmise inflation plays. The reason is that *real growth takes time*. To increase unit sales, a business must expand production, build a new factory or factories, add new outlets, and set up a sales force in new markets. These require advance planning and time to bear fruit. Because real growth takes time, a business that is expecting to grow in real terms needs the use of borrowed money for as long as possible. It can't implement its plans overnight. Thus, a short-term loan, one that must be repaid quickly, doesn't serve the purpose of a business that is expecting to grow in real terms. For this reason, when businesses in general are anticipating real growth, they are willing to incur slightly higher interest costs in return for having the use of the loan for a longer period of time. And since interest rates reflect demand, under these circumstances long-term rates will remain above short-term rates.

Given the relationship between interest rates and growth, it follows that one of the most unstable of all economic environments prevails when short-term rates rise above long-term rates. This condition, known as an *inverted yield curve,* tells you that shorter-term growth is easier to come by than growth over the longer term. And it invariably means that something is seriously out of whack with the economy.

It's a little bit as if your pediatrician tells you that in

six months your son, now 3 feet tall, will be 3 feet 6 inches, but that in a year he will be only 3 feet 4 inches tall. You would know that something is seriously wrong. So it is with the economy whenever short-term rates rise above long-term rates.

The powerful implication is that if short-term rates rise above long-term rates, the outlook is for *negative real growth*. This will become clear if you plug in some numbers. Suppose short-term rates are 10% and long-term rates higher at 11%. You can deduce that inflation is expected to be no more than 10%, and that real growth, therefore, is expected to be at least 1%—that is, positive.

By contrast, suppose that short-term rates, at 12%, are higher than long-term rates at 10%. Since a good part of that 12% represents inflationary expectations, it is likely that 100% or more of the 10% comes from inflation. And this means that the real growth portion must be 0 or negative.*

It is important to remember that when Condition No. 3 is in place, it doesn't *necessarily* mean that you can count on positive real growth or on a bull market. The prime example of a positive ratio remaining blithely, insouciantly, operative in the face of economic disaster was the Great Depression. Throughout the 1930s long-term rates, which averaged about 3.9%, remained firmly above short-term rates, averaging below 1%.

---

*Short-term rates are not purely and simply a proxy for inflation—if they were, we'd be facing inflation of 7% to 8% now, which isn't the case. In today's world, short-term rates may incorporate a little bit more real growth than in the past. The reason is that during the past decade our economy has become increasingly service-oriented as opposed to goods-oriented—and real growth can be generated faster in services than in goods. But this does not alter the underlying relationships. Shorter-term rates are more reflective of inflation than are longer-term rates.

There is an explanation for this apparent inconsistency. During the 1930s, and indeed up until the 1960s, whenever the country sank into depression or recession, the downturn was always accompanied by negative inflation—by *deflation*. And in this kind of economy, my third condition simply isn't relevant. *The ratio of long-term to short-term rates is meaningful as an indicator only when the danger is of negative real growth in the context of positive inflation.* In other words, as long as real growth is expected to be positive, long-term rates—which reflect both growth and inflation—will be higher than short-term rates, which reflect mostly inflation.

That is why this condition was in place almost without interruption from the early 1920s on through the mid-1960s. During those years, the threat to growth was not so much inflation as deflation, a shortage of money. When real growth was negative, it was always in the context of negative inflation. So, during the first part of the century, Condition No. 3 was not an important factor. True, it was in place during both secular bull markets, but since it was nearly always in place, this wasn't too significant.

Only since the mid-1960s has the economy functioned in such a way as to periodically suffer prolonged periods of negative growth coupled with rising prices. Thus, Condition No. 3 has become a critical indicator only quite recently. But if its history in that sense is short, it has made up for it with a vengeance, for once it started to give buy and sell signals, it has done so with great accuracy.

For starters, short-term rates were above long-term rates throughout the two most vicious recent bear markets. From February 1969 through June 1970, the S&P

400 fell from 110.20 to 82.46, or by nearly 25%. And from May 1973 to December 1974 the S&P 400 fell from 120.00 to 74.80, a nearly 38% drop. During the former period, short-term rates, as measured by Fed funds, averaged 8.4%, while long-term rates, as measured by S&P-rated AAA bonds, averaged 7.2%. In the latter period, short-term rates averaged 10.3% and long-term rates 8.0%. Moreover, during both these periods *there was not a single month in which long-term rates exceeded short-term rates.* And, consistent with my theory, both periods were characterized by rapid inflation in the context of negative growth.

These examples are striking evidence of the value of this indicator. But there are other ways, as well, to assess its overall record.

One approach is to look at those times when the ratio moved below 1—when short-term rates exceeded long-term rates. The first time this happened after 1929 was in June 1966, exactly as the second secular bull market was winding to a close. Using this date as a starting point, it is possible to construct a very simple rule: *Buy stocks only when the ratio of long-term to short-term rates is above 1, and sell whenever the ratio drops below 1.*

Figure 5-1 summarizes the results of following the signals from this one indicator.

As with Condition No. 2, what we have here is not just an indicator that can predict secular bull markets, but one that is also exceedingly useful in predicting intermediate-term market turns. An investor who had remained continuously invested in the S&P 400 from August 1966 through mid-1985 would have made gains of 118%, or 4.2% on an annualized basis. By contrast, an investor who had religiously followed the signals of my third condition, buying when the indicator turned positive and selling when it turned negative, would have racked up gains of 337% over the same period, or 12% a year.

A second way to make use of my third condition—even during those times when the ratio of long-term to short-term rates remains above 1—is to look at the *trend* of the ratio. Or, to put it differently, to look at the peaks in the ratio of long-term to short-term rates in relation to peaks in stocks.* (See Figure 5-2.)

It turns out that *every significant market decline—a drop of 10% or more in the S&P 400—in the past thirty years followed, by various time lags, a peak in the ratio.* In other words, as long as the spread between short-term and long-term rates was widening—meaning that the expectation was for real growth to gain on inflation—the stock market would continue to rise. Only when the spread between short-term and long-term rates began narrowing—when the ratio started falling—was there a danger that the market would come down in a big way.

A rising ratio of long-term to short-term rates, then, is a sign that real growth is gaining on inflation. It is a positive omen for the bull.

There is one further way to make use of Condition No. 3. At a certain point, if the ratio is rising *too* rapidly, it can also be seen as a warning that a turnaround may not be far off. The reason is that *real growth cannot keep expanding indefinitely.* A moderate level of growth can be sustained for long periods of time, but if the expecta-

---

*To avoid the occasional random fluctuation, I have found it best when defining peaks to use a six-month average of the ratio rather than simply following month-to-month changes.

**FIGURE 5-1**

## RESULTS OF BUY SIGNALS
## FROM THE LONG-SHORT INDICATOR

| Dates When Ratio Was Above 1 | Behavior of S&P 400 | % Gain or Loss |
|---|---|---|
| 8/66 to 10/66 | 86.40 to 82.01 | − 5.1 |
| 12/66 to 8/68 | 86.50 to 106.80 | + 23.5 |
| 9/68 to 2/69 | 110.50 to 110.20 | − 0.3 |
| 6/70 to 5/73 | 82.96 to 120.00 | + 44.7 |
| 12/74 to 10/78 | 74.80 to 111.60 | + 49.2 |
| 6/80 to 10/80 | 128.80 to 148.40 | + 15.2 |
| 10/81 to 5/82 | 134.00 to 122.85 | − 8.3 |
| 6/82 to May 1985 | 122.61 to 202.13 | + 64.0 |

Gain from being invested only when ratio was above 1: 337% (annualized gain of 12%).
Gain from being continuously invested: 118% (annualized gain of 4.2%).

tions are for real growth of 4% one quarter, 5% the next, 6% the next, and so on, the expectations will almost invariably be disappointed. If long-term rates are rising too fast relative to short-term rates, it is exceedingly likely that at some point growth will slow. The spread will start to narrow dramatically. And this reversal—even if it doesn't lead to an outright sell signal—can be a sign that the market is headed for a tumble.

This is particularly true since it often happens that a rapidly rising ratio of long to short rates can go hand in

FIGURE 5-2

## RATIO OF LONG TO SHORT RATES
## IN RELATION TO STOCK MARKET PEAKS*

| Market Peak | | Ratio Peak | | Months Between Ratio Peak |
|---|---|---|---|---|
| *S&P 400* | *Date* | *Date* | *Level* | *and S&P Peak* |
| 52.27 | 7/56 | 6/54 | 2.20 | 25 |
| 75.81 | 12/61 | 9/61 | 2.66 | 3 |
| 99.56 | 1/66 | 10/64 | 1.27 | 15 |
| 116.00 | 12/68 | 11/67 | 1.45 | 13 |
| 132.60 | 1/73 | 5/72 | 1.89 | 8 |
| 118.20 | 9/76 | 5/76 | 1.72 | 4 |
| 155.10 | 11/80 | 10/80 | 1.07 | 1 |
| 189.00 | 10/83 | 9/83 | 1.28 | 1 |

*Uses 6-month moving average of ratio.

hand with rising speculation in the market. The explanation is that both a rising ratio and speculation imply that expectations—about growth in general and about the stock market or particular kinds of stocks—have become too heated. You are being given a clear warning that a break may be at hand. When the ratio starts to fall, you are getting an even clearer warning that the break is right at hand, and it's time to take action.

A prime example of this was the vicious correction of 1962, when the market, having risen by nearly 70% between December 1957 and January 1962, fell more than 25% in four months. At that time Conditions No. 1 and 2 remained firmly in place. This was strong reassurance that on a long-term basis the secular bull was

## FIGURE 5-3

# AAA Bonds/Fed Funds
### 6-Month M.A.

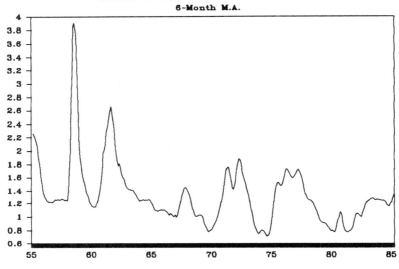

## FIGURE 5-4

# S&P 400

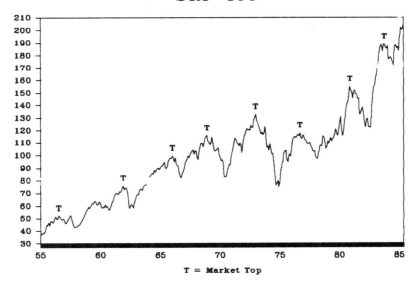

T = Market Top

alive and well. But anyone alert to Condition No. 3 would have noted that by January 1962 the spread between long-term and short-term rates had narrowed drastically: While long-term rates remained in the 4.3% area for quite a while, short-term rates rose from under 1.5% in June 1961 to over 2% by January 1962. The rapid narrowing of the spread was a strong sign that a correction was brewing.

But something else was going on in 1962 as well. This was a time of freewheeling speculation, particularly in the technology stocks, but also in the market as a whole. It is no coincidence, I think, that heavy speculation went hand in hand with a peak in this ratio. A peak in the ratio means, by definition, that expectations of growth are also at a peak. When the ratio starts to decline, it is like someone suddenly perceiving that his or her lover has flaws that, in the first few weeks or months of passion, had not been apparent. A period of disillusionment follows. But if the relationship has some solid underpinnings, it will survive—as will a bull market that is based on solid growth, once the speculative excesses are surmounted.

Condition No. 3 has been positive—the ratio of long-term to short-term rates has remained above 1—since June 1982. But even in the relatively short period since then in which the bull has been charging, there has been one correction. From October 1983 through July 1984 the S&P 400 (based on monthly averages) fell by almost 10%. Did the ratio provide any hint that it was coming? Yes. Prior to the correction the spread between long-term and short-term rates narrowed. As in 1962, this correction also came on the heels of a speculative burst. In mid-1983 virtually any new issue was guaranteed to double or triple in price within weeks. Stocks with no earnings were being gobbled up at sky-high premiums—such names as Victor Technologies, Tele-Video, and Diasonics spring to mind. Once again, a declining ratio and heavy speculation were a powerful one-two punch that knocked the market for a correction. But again, the fact that the ratio still remained above 1 meant that the market did not go down for the count and that the secular bull remained alive.

Condition No. 3, then, provides one more piece of evidence that the bull market that began in 1982 is in no danger of flagging. And together, Conditions No. 2 and 3 prove that interest rates, just as everyone thinks, do count. The problem is that most people focus on the wrong things.

*To know if the bull is going to be around for a while, don't look at whether rates are rising or falling—look at rates in relation to inflation, as Condition No. 2 tells you.* And to get some advance warning as to any temporary or more serious break in the market, again, don't worry about the direction of rates, keep your eyes fixed on the relationship of long-term to short-term rates.

# 6

# THE MEANING OF MONEY

***Condition No. 4:*** *The money supply must be growing.*

Money makes the world go 'round; money is the root of all evil; money is that thing than which love may or may not be more important.

Or whatever. Money, for better or worse, has occupied the thoughts and influenced the actions of countless people down through the ages. But what exactly is money, and how does it fit into the scheme of things in today's complicated economy? There is surprisingly little agreement among economists.

My view is that while an adequately growing money supply is essential to economic growth and, therefore, to bull markets, money—contrary to monetarist dogma—is *not* the one and only determinant of everything that happens in our economy. In particular, while the monetarists believe that monetary policy is the be-all and end-all when it comes to predicting the future course of inflation—that an oversupply of money is *the* cause of inflation—I have serious doubts about that easy formula.

But before we look at why the monetarists are wrong about inflation, let's first show why money is essential to economic growth—i.e., why we need Condition No. 4. Economists have come up with various definitions of money. These involve the infamous Ms, having to do with how readily spendable various types of money are.

• M1 is the most spendable. It consists of cash in circulation and those instruments that most closely resemble cash—demand deposits in commercial banks, NOW interest-paying checking accounts, ATS (automatic transfer from savings) accounts, credit union share drafts, mutual savings bank demand deposits, and nonbank traveler's checks.

• M2 as a whole is a little less spendable. It consists of all the above, plus such items as savings accounts, overnight Eurodollars, money market mutual fund shares, overnight repurchase agreements issued by commercial banks, and time deposits under $100,000.

• M3 goes into even loftier realms: It encompasses everything in M2 as well as time deposits over $100,000 and term repurchase agreements.

• Finally, there is something called L, which most people haven't even heard of. It takes in all the above plus Treasury bills, savings bonds, commercial paper, bankers' acceptances, and nonbank Eurodollar holdings of U.S. residents.

But no matter what definition you use, the following equation is always true: MV = GNP, where M stands for money, V stands for velocity, and GNP for the Gross National Product. This equation, which is as basic as

$2 + 2 = 4$, goes far toward explaining why money is so important to growth.

Here's an easy way of understanding exactly what the equation means. Imagine that you have been marooned on an island with one other person. You're an expert at using your hands to build things; his forte is planting and gardening. So you assume responsibility for shelter, tools, etc.; he takes charge of producing food. Now imagine that you find in your pocket a single dollar bill; your compatriot has nothing. You launch your island economy by purchasing a tomato from your friend for $1. He in turn gives the $1 back to you in exchange for a nicely sanded piece of wood. And so on and so forth. By the end of a year the dollar has exchanged hands 685 times, which is what is meant by velocity, and your island's Gross National Product can be toted up as $685.

On a much grander scale this is exactly what the Gross National Product of the United States represents: the total amount of money multiplied by the number of times it changes hands. And this is a useful definition indeed, for it tells us that the only way the economy can grow is if the money supply grows. True, if the money supply were to contract, the economy could still grow— if velocity were to pick up. But this rarely happens. Typically, when the supply of money starts to fall, velocity also falls or at least remains about the same. Essentially, as money becomes scarcer, people become less willing to spend what they have—they tend to save more, which leads to reduced velocity. Thus, a slowdown in the money supply nearly always results in a slowdown in economic growth.

As a result fluctuations in the money supply have been a key economic indicator. One example is the very early 1930s, when a declining money supply foretold that the economic downturn would not be ephemeral. And in 1933—and 1950—growth in the money supply could have told anyone attuned to my four conditions that severe economic distress was coming to an end and that it was time to get back in the market.

In the post–World War II period the money supply has been in an almost continuous uptrend, with only a few minor interruptions. And that accounts in large measure for the fact that since World War II, while there have been many recessions, there have been no prolonged periods of economic contraction—nothing on a par with what happened in the early 1930s, for example. The reason is that during this period the relationship between money and growth has become better understood, and the Fed has been unwilling to let the money supply decline for any lengthy period of time.

Thus, my fourth condition, an increase in the money supply, was far more important as a forecasting tool during the first half of the twentieth century than it was thirty years ago or today. Nonetheless, it behooves us to keep a close eye on this factor, one reason being that some benighted Fed chairman, alarmed by the possibility of runaway inflation, might panic, tighten the monetary screws too hard, and send the economy—and the market—into a prolonged tailspin. In that case, knowing how to read the signals could pull you out of the market intact.

Moreover, understanding the key role of money supply can let you know when *not* to worry about a host of economic problems. Today, for example, you read a lot about the farm crisis, the Third World debt crisis, and the crisis in international trade. But these problems, however serious in their own right, pose no threat to economic growth or the secular bull—not as long as the money supply continues growing. During the wildly prosperous 1920s there also was a severe farm crisis, and banks that made loans to farms failed at the rate of 635 a year during that decade, compared with only 88 failures a year over the previous twenty years. But the farm crisis did not spread to the rest of the economy because the money supply remained in a steady uptrend. It is no different today: As long as the money supply continues to grow the economy can remain on a strong growth path.

Finally, knowing how to interpret trends in the money supply correctly—something that most economists seem incapable of doing—can tell us when economic growth will continue to be vigorous and when it will lag, with obvious implications for making profits from the stock market. It can also calm our fears about a temporary flareup in inflation.

Even though Condition No. 4 is, today, not as important as the first three in predicting the onset of a secular bull market, do not ignore it when making your predictions.

How can you tell if money supply is on an upward trend, and how much of an uptrend is sufficient? To answer this, I have developed what I call the Rule of 3s, which says that growth in the money supply* is on an

---

*Money supply in this case would be M2.

uptrend *if for three consecutive months the three-month average of the money supply is higher than the average of the previous three months.* (See Figure 6-1.)

**FIGURE 6-1**

## The Rule of 3s

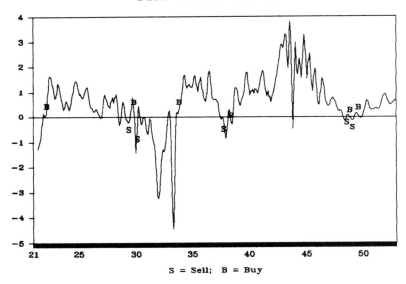

S = Sell;  B = Buy

That's quite a mouthful, but it's really pretty easy to understand. Suppose that from January through March the money supply averaged $500 billion, compared to an average of $450 billion for the three months from October through December. That's considered one month of an uptrend, March. Now suppose that the February through April average is higher than the November through January average; that makes two consecutive months of an uptrend: March and April. Finally, suppose that the March through May average

98

is higher than the December through February figure; that makes three consecutive months of rising money supply according to my definition and allows us to say that money supply is in a definite uptrend.

When everything is reversed—when you have three consecutive months of decline, again using three-month averages—you can conclude that the money supply is in a definite downtrend.

Why such a seemingly complicated rule? Because it helps to determine when a change in the money supply is meaningful and when it is just a random fluctuation. Sure, if you look at the long-term chart of money supply growth, it's easy to point to periods in which the money supply started advancing and declining. But that's because you know what comes next. When you don't know what lies ahead it's another matter. You need some kind of rule that enables you to identify significant changes. The Rule of 3s does this. However, it is certainly not the only way to go about defining uptrends and downtrends. If you were to follow other rules, such as looking just at three consecutive months of money supply growth, you would obtain similar results. The advantage to the Rule of 3s is that it gives somewhat smoother, more refined readings.*

How would an investor who followed the Rule of 3s— and *no other indicator*—have fared in the 1921–1949 period? Very well. Figure 6-2 shows that during those twenty-eight years my Rule of 3s gave eleven signals. Ten of them were correct. But even this summary is a bit misleading, for the one wrong signal missed by just a

---

*To ensure further that an uptrend or downtrend in the money supply is significant, I require that in at least one of the three months money must be growing or declining by at least 0.1%.

FIGURE 6-2

## SIGNALS FROM THE RULE OF 3s

| Signal Date | Signal | DJIA | % Change from Signal* |
|---|---|---|---|
| Feb 1922 | Buy | 89.05 | +275% |
| May 1929 | Sell | 333.79 | + 28 |
| Oct 1929 | Buy | 238.95 | + 20 |
| Feb 1930 | Sell | 286.10 | + 66 |
| Oct 1933 | Buy | 98.14 | + 41 |
| Sept 1937 | Sell | 138.17 | + 3 |
| May 1938 | Buy | 133.88 | + 36 |
| July 1948 | Sell | 181.71 | + 6 |
| Oct 1948 | Buy | 171.20 | + 1 |
| Jan 1949 | Sell | 173.06 | − 3 |
| July 1949 | Buy | 178.66 | |
| Compounded Gain | . . . . . . . . . . . . . . . . . . . . . . . . | | +1860% |

*Assumes buying stocks when signal is positive and shorting stocks when signal is negative and assumes that you act on signal at the end of the month *following* the one in which the signal occurred.

small amount, while the right ones were by and large humdingers. Altogether, the investor would have realized a compounded gain of nearly 1900% as compared with less than 100% by staying in the market continuously.

But before you start thinking that this is all ancient history, and that the money supply doesn't count for much in today's economy, consider the following: In October 1984 economists were in almost universal accord that 1985 would be a bang-up year. Robert

100

Eggert's so-called blue-chip economists, for example—leading forecasters from both corporations and academia—predicted that the economy would advance by 3.5%. In fact, the first half of 1985 witnessed economic growth of below 1% on an annual basis. Having erred on the side of gloom the last time around, completely missing the slam-bang recovery of 1982, economists once again crammed into the wrong boat.

A simple equation involving money supply growth told me at the time that the pundits were being far too optimistic. The equation says that when real growth in the money supply (money supply minus inflation) is greater than real growth, it is likely that the following year will be a strong one for the economy. Conversely, when real money growth is less than real growth, as was the case in 1984, the following year is likely to be a poor one for the economy.

When there is more than enough money to support growth, some of that money spurs growth in the following year. By the same token, when there is too little money to support growth, in the following year there will be a relative shortage of money, and growth will slow.

Over the past thirty years this simple theory has produced dramatically accurate results in terms of predicting the performance of the economy and the stock market alike. Figures 6-3 and 6-4 summarize the results, showing that when money growth was greater than growth in the GNP, the following year the economy on average grew a brisk 6.00%, while the market advanced some 10.57%. When money growth was below growth in the GNP, the following year saw economic growth of only 1.24% and a market advance of 3.87%.

**FIGURE 6-3**

# BASIC DATA ON MONEY SUPPLY GROWTH AND GNP GROWTH SINCE 1955

| Year | GNP Growth | % Change in in S&P 400 | Real M2 Less GNP in Previous Year* |
|------|------------|------------------------|------------------------------------|
| 1983 | 6.35% | 35.10% | 5.08 |
| 1955 | 7.62 | 40.17 | 4.51 |
| 1972 | 5.70 | 12.36 | 4.14 |
| 1962 | 6.56 | − 6.36 | 3.68 |
| 1973 | 5.80 | − 1.07 | 3.19 |
| 1959 | 6.39 | 24.49 | 3.16 |
| 1964 | 5.46 | 17.44 | 3.11 |
| 1984 | 6.80 | 0.42 | 2.80 |
| 1977 | 5.50 | − 5.16 | 1.41 |
| 1968 | 4.65 | 8.38 | 1.32 |
| 1976 | 5.40 | 18.37 | 1.28 |
| 1965 | 6.32 | 8.46 | 0.96 |
| 1978 | 5.00 | − 2.03 | 0.33 |
| 1966 | 6.52 | − 2.56 | 0.08 |
| 1963 | 4.00 | 11.98 | − 0.05 |
| 1961 | 1.95 | 17.77 | − 0.27 |
| 1969 | 2.56 | − 0.33 | − 0.78 |
| 1971 | 3.40 | 18.74 | − 1.02 |
| 1960 | 2.48 | − 3.29 | − 1.27 |
| 1957 | 1.43 | − 4.36 | − 1.61 |
| 1970 | − 0.65 | − 14.79 | − 1.74 |
| 1958 | − 1.15 | 3.63 | − 2.16 |
| 1974 | − 0.60 | − 22.90 | − 2.28 |
| 1967 | 2.60 | 8.88 | − 3.08 |
| 1982 | − 1.90 | − 7.42 | − 3.43 |

| Year | GNP Growth | % Change in in S&P 400 | Real M2 Less GNP in Previous Year* |
|------|-----------|----------------------|-----------------------------------|
| 1956 | 1.85 | 17.45 | −3.62 |
| 1975 | −1.20 | 3.93 | −3.80 |
| 1979 | 2.80 | 8.10 | −4.14 |
| 1981 | 2.60 | 7.29 | −4.50 |
| 1980 | −0.30 | 17.16 | −5.47 |

*Real M2 = Actual M2 Growth − Inflation.

**FIGURE 6-4**

## SUMMARY OF DATA

| Relationship | Average Change in Real Growth | Average Change in S&P 400 |
|--------------|------------------------------|--------------------------|
| M Greater than GNP | +6.00% | +10.57% |
| M Less than GNP | +1.24 | + 3.87 |

One of the nice things about this equation relating money supply growth and GNP is that you don't need a million-dollar supercomputer to make your prediction. You need only a few numbers—GNP growth, inflation, and money growth—all of which are obtainable from sources such as *The Wall Street Journal* or *Barron's*. In a few moments you can come up with your own calculation as to the pace of future economic growth, and, as the example of 1984 shows, it is likely to give you a leg up on some of the highest-paid economists around.

One more point: It is commonly accepted that there is a strong relationship between money growth and inflation—or at least the monetarists think so. Specifically, they hold that when the money supply grows too rapidly, the inevitable result is a surge in inflation.

The widespread acceptance of this belief is why in the early 1980s, for example, Fed-watching became a weekly ritual on Wall Street. Whenever the Fed reported that the money supply had grown faster than expected, investors panicked. They assumed inflation was heating up—and that the Fed therefore would be forced to tighten. So they phoned in sell orders.

But there is no better counterexample than the early 1980s themselves. Between 1980 and 1985 inflation fell from double-digit levels to well below 5%, and to 1% in terms of producer prices. Was money supply growth slow during this period? No, just the opposite. Between 1981 and 1984—just as the back of inflation was being broken—the money supply was growing by around 10%. The monetarists were baffled, but valiantly stuck to their guns, repeatedly forecasting a return to high inflation.

They were wrong on numerous occasions, but there is always the strong possibility that double-digit inflation will once again be with us, and then monetarists and their cousins, the gold bugs, will be able to say that they were right all along. (In the prediction business, as long as you are consistently bullish or bearish, you will ultimately be vindicated!)

The events of the past several years indicate that a rapid growth in the money supply does not automatically *lead to* a rapid increase in the inflation rate. However, it is usually true that a rapid increase in the inflation rate is *accompanied by* a rapid growth in the money supply.

104

So, if prices are rising at a fast clip, and you look in the financial pages and see that money supply has also been moving right along, you can deduce that inflation is a thorny problem that augurs trouble for both the economy and the stock market.

Sometimes, though, there can be an eruption of inflation that is not accompanied by rapid money supply growth. And this circumstance lets you know that the inflation is likely to be a temporary condition that will inflict no lasting harm on either the economy or the stock market. A perfect example is what happened during the Korean War. In 1951 most measures of inflation shot up, turning Condition No. 2 negative, primarily because of transitory shortages in various commodities. Inflation was a marginal, not a structural problem. How could investors at the time have known this, and known to stay in the market? By looking at the behavior of the money supply: It grew by less than 3% in 1951— nothing to get alarmed about. And by 1952 inflation was once again at a moderate level.

To summarize what you need to know about money: Long-term bull markets require that money supply growth be on an uptrend, as measured by the Rule of 3s. During the last thirty years, the supply of money has been generally increasing, but money is still a good predictor of both economic growth and stock market performance. For example, when money supply grows faster in one year than the GNP does, then economic growth is likely to be strong the following year and stocks should rise significantly.

Finally, despite what most economists think, rapid money supply growth does *not* necessarily lead to rapid inflation. But because rapid inflation *does* usually lead to rapid money supply growth, a spurt in prices that is not accompanied by rapid money supply growth tells you that the inflation is transitory.

So, just as your mother undoubtedly told you, money does count. Its fluctuating presence in the economy isn't something to be shunted aside in making your investment decisions. But the amount of money in circulation cannot, as so many economists believe, be held entirely responsible for either the curse of uncontrollable inflation or the blessing of relatively stable prices.

For the economy, as for an individual, there is probably some ideal amount of money that is just right. But too much money sure beats the hell out of too little. Money is great, and I hope this book helps you make more of it.

# 7

# THE SYSTEM AT WORK

My grandfather, orphaned at ten and a self-made millionaire at thirty-five (he made his money in the furniture business and had a lifelong distrust of the stock market), stood five feet two in his bare feet and had a short temper to match. He was constantly asking, "Am I right or am I wrong?" To him there was no middle ground. He detested ambiguity, demanding black-and-white certainty in everything he did.

It's probably good that he stayed away from stocks, because in the market there is no such thing as absolute certainty. There is always the need for interpretation, for an ability to weigh varying possibilities and make a choice. And you will never be 100% right.

The four fundamental conditions I have given you correlate strongly with sustainable economic growth and secular bull markets and are the best guides I know of for telling you when you should put everything you own into stocks, holding on through thick and thin in the knowledge that over the long run you will make a fortune. However, it should be clear by now that they do require a little thought and interpretation. They are not quite as good as a magic talisman that grows warm in your pocket just as the secular bull market is starting and cools off as the bull expires. Sometimes some of the conditions are in place, but not others, and you have to analyze the situation to figure out which ones to heed.

Moreover, when it comes to applying these conditions in real life, you are suddenly faced with certain nitty-gritty problems. For example, which particular measure of inflation should you use—consumer prices, producer prices, or some other? When it comes to short-term interest rates, which ones should count most— T-bills, Fed funds, or the discount rate? And, if one or two of the conditions are positive and the others negative, which ones do you go by? How does everything fit together?

To give you a better idea of how to go about applying my conditions—and to convince you that they really do work—let us go through the stock market since the beginning of the 1920s, to see exactly how they would have directed investment decisions at each moment. Let us imagine an investor whom we will call Jonas Dowe. Jonas was born with the century, and thus when 1921 dawned he had just turned twenty-one. Suppose I have been able to go back in time and have confided in Jonas the secret of my four conditions. Suppose further that on his twenty-first birthday Jonas came into an inheritance of $10,000. Being a game sort of guy, and regarding this as found money, he was perfectly willing to put it in the stock market as my four conditions dictated. And finally, to keep matters simple, suppose that Jonas

108

was somehow able to invest his funds in the Dow Jones Industrial Average rather than in individual stocks.

As 1921 opened, my ratio of real growth to inflation was above 1, but only because real growth was declining at a lesser rate than prices were falling. My two interest rate indicators were in place—with prices declining by 10%, inflation was obviously less than half of bond yields, and virtually all short-term rates were below long-term rates—but the money supply was contracting. Consulting the list of conditions that I had left with him, Jonas correctly decided that there was still no indication that a resumption of economic growth was imminent and that it was not yet time to get into the market.

In August something happened that gave Jonas a brief start: The money supply rose for the month. It was a small rise, 3.4% on an annualized basis, but it was the first indication that the recession might be ending. In that prices were still declining, real money growth also rose. Thus, at the most primitive level, the four conditions all coalesced at almost precisely the moment that the first great secular bull market of the century was getting off the ground.

However, a one-month spurt in the money supply isn't sufficient to put Condition No. 4 into place. Following that one-month rise in August, money supply growth flattened out; while the downtrend had been definitively broken, an uptrend did not start in earnest until the first quarter of 1922. So, in late March 1922, when the Dow was in the high 80s, Jonas committed his $10,000 to the market.

All four conditions remained in place without letup for the next six years, until the end of 1928. True, in

1927 and in the early part of 1928, real economic growth turned briefly negative—something that led some people at the time to warn that the bull market's days were numbered. But Jonas wasn't concerned. With prices still declining, the ratio of real growth to inflation remained above 1, and money supply growth remained steadily up, reassuring Jonas that the economic downturn was just temporary.

But by the end of 1928 there were signs that things might be going a bit awry. Condition No. 3 was a little shaky. Some short-term rates had started to rise relative to some long-term rates, and the discount rate at 5% was above long-term bond yields, as were commercial paper rates, which were also in the 5% vicinity. On the plus side, however, the yields from short-term T-bills— there were no Fed funds at the time—remained below bond yields. Jonas was a little worried, but he decided that since the other conditions were in place, he would not sell.

In March 1929, however, the money supply started to contract. The decline continued in April and in May, marking the first time since the bull market began that there had been three consecutive months of falling money supply. Condition No. 4 was no longer in place—and that was enough to convince Jonas that it was time to take cover. He got out of the market in late June 1929, with the Dow at 333.8.

Yes, he missed the last 50 or so points and he had to endure a lot of ribbing from his friends, who stayed on for the final portion of the market's wild ride. But his portfolio had appreciated from $10,000 to $48,703. And, even more to the point, he had gotten out before the Crash.

In November he briefly re-entered the market: Aggressive actions by the Federal Reserve immediately following the Crash pumped up the money supply to the point where the Rule of 3s gave a buy signal. And while many short-term rates were still above long-term rates, T-bills—the most significant measure of short-term rates—were below long-term rates. Jonas remained in the market until March 1930, when money supply growth again turned decisively negative, by which time his portfolio had climbed to nearly $61,000.

So much for the Roaring Twenties. In the early 1930s a judicious interpretation of my conditions kept Jonas resolutely out of the market. True, the interest rate conditions were then in place, while for a few scattered months in 1930 the money supply rose. But there never were three consecutive months of growth in the money supply. Also, during that year our ratio was below 1, as real growth fell by nearly 10%, as against about a 3% drop in prices.

It was not until late 1933 that Jonas once again entered the fray, in time to capitalize on the mini secular bull market that began that year. By that time his portfolio, which since early 1930 had been parked in high-grade corporate bonds, yielding about 4.5% on average, had grown to $85,937. The first three conditions had all been in place for some time, though of course, in light of the Depression, the ratio of real growth to inflation was above 1 in the context of declining real growth. All that Jonas was waiting for was a growing money supply. From June through October the money supply grew steadily, and Jonas got back into the market with the Dow at 98.1.

111

Except for a brief period during 1934, all four conditions remained in place for the next several years. The condition that broke down in 1934 was the relationship between long-term bond yields and inflation: Prices started rising faster than twice what bonds were yielding. The reason was a series of disastrous dust storms and droughts, which pushed food prices way up. Did Jonas realize that the surge in inflation that threw the condition out of whack was destined to be short-lived? Maybe, maybe not. For convenience, let's say he did; it doesn't affect the results much, one way or the other. Jonas stayed in the market through 1936.

But in January 1937, with the Dow in the 180s, Jonas took one look at the state of the conditions and with a shudder withdrew his money—which by then had grown to $184,981—from the market. A good thing, too, since the DJIA, after rising briefly, plummeted to below 120 by December. What alerted Jonas was that inflation had risen to where it actually exceeded long-term rates. Real rates, in other words, were negative, and the first interest-rate condition was flashing an emphatic sell signal. By the middle of the year, money supply growth began to decline, and by the end of the year economic growth turned negative and was less than inflation, bringing our ratio below 1. The only condition that held for the year was that long-term interest rates exceeded short-term rates—but, as we have seen, until the mid-1960s this condition was not particularly relevant.

The following year, however, began on a better note. Prices were falling, and while the economy was still contracting, the money supply during January climbed at an 8.1% annualized rate. Subsequently, the money supply backed off again, however, and it wasn't until fall that the fourth condition joined the first three in the positive fold, giving Jonas the signal he needed to move back into stocks. His portfolio then was valued at $208,041.

In September 1939 World War II began. The war was to have a multilayered effect on the economy, even before the U.S. officially entered it in late 1941. The most striking effect was the steep rise in inflation, which from 1941 through 1946 averaged more than 7%. Moreover, in 1942 the government officially imposed controls on interest rates. With inflation high and interest rates low—though artificially so—my conditions did not hold during much of the war years, and Jonas, his portfolio worth $238,207, was out of stocks by January 1940.

As it turned out, this was not the wisest decision. True, the early war years were tough going for the market, with the Dow declining from 150 in January 1940 to 93 by April 1942. But then the market rallied strongly to over 210 by June 1946, a move that Jonas missed entirely.

Had my conditions failed? I don't think so. Remember, during the years we are talking about, the government had imposed stringent controls to keep interest rates down. My conditions are based on a relatively free marketplace, the only kind that can accurately reflect supply and demand and hence expectations of growth. It is true that even in peacetime the Fed controls the money supply to some extent, but always in response to what it perceives to be the needs of the markets to continue to function in an economically fluid fashion. With far more severe constraints present during the war years, my conditions ceased to function as meaningful guides.

Jonas remained out of the market and in bonds for several more years. Even after the war ended, inflation remained high, and the ratio was bearish. In 1946, in fact, the difference between real growth and inflation was a staggering 22 percentage points: Prices were rising by 11% while real growth was declining by 11%. The economy looked almost as bleak in 1947, as prices continued to climb at a double-digit rate while real growth continued negative. Things improved in 1948 as growth turned solidly positive; the economy expanded at a 4.5% rate. But inflation, by most measures close to 7%, remained uncomfortably high.

In 1949 inflation vanished from the economic scene, and the first interest rate condition moved into place. But along with this decline came an economic contraction. Before getting back into the market, Jonas needed proof, in the form of positive growth in the money supply, that the economy was not headed for an open-ended decline. And by March the money supply not only stopped declining but began to rise. By August the Rule of 3s finally gave a buy signal. And one month later Jonas, for the first time in a decade, was back in the stock market. His portfolio was worth $354,739. The Dow was at 178.7, only a few points above a multi-year low, and the second full-fledged secular bull market was just getting off the ground.

All four conditions remained unambiguously in place through June 1950, when the Korean War broke out. (See Figure 7-1.) Then fear of shortages and hoarding led to a sharp rise in producer (wholesale) prices, turning Condition No. 2 negative. The other conditions were satisfied in spades as the economy grew at a nearly 10% rate. During 1951 and the first half of 1952, again, the only problem was the second condition, as inflation stayed above half the yield of bonds.

**FIGURE 7-1**

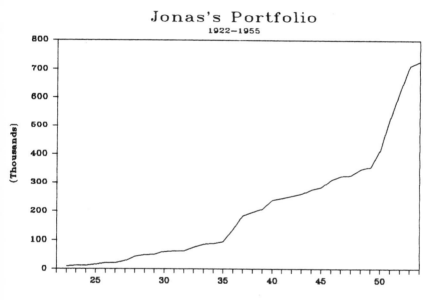

Jonas's Portfolio
1922–1955

The question Jonas had to answer was whether this inflation was a temporary blip that resulted from the war and from the economic controls passed in July and September 1950 or a more permanent problem. He decided it was the former because of one crucial difference between the early 1950s and the high-inflation 1942–1946 period. In the 1950s money supply growth did not run riot as it had done in the 1940s. In the

115

earlier period money growth averaged a torrid 19% a year. In the early 1950s money supply grew by only 3½% a year on average, which told Jonas that the economy was not likely to get overheated. With the ratio of real growth to inflation above 1 and the third and fourth conditions comfortably satisfied, Jonas stayed in the market.

In 1954 the economy experienced a brief contraction. Though the ratio fell below 1, inflation remained very moderate, around 1%, and the other conditions were all satisfied. The fact that the money supply continued to grow steadily indicated the contraction would be brief, and Jonas, by now an old pro at this, remained in stocks with hardly a qualm.

In April 1956 he got out. The DJIA had climbed all the way to 518.0 by then, and Jonas's portfolio was valued at $1,459,857. What made him get out was the failure of Condition No. 2: Long-term interest rates had dropped to below twice the inflation rate, regardless of what measure of inflation was used. As opposed to the early 1950s, this time there were no extraordinary circumstances to account for the rise in prices. Moreover, unlike the Korean War period, all measures of inflation had risen above real growth, turning Condition No. 1 negative. Inflation appeared to be getting the upper hand.

By 1958 there was some evidence of improvement. In March of that year the economy was emerging from a mild recession. The money supply, which had been declining in late 1957, had been growing for three months, and long-term rates were well above short-term rates. In particular, long-term rates were more than twice producer prices (then called wholesale prices), though still not more than twice consumer price changes. Jonas knew that producer prices should logically lead consumer prices.* As a result, Jonas felt he could afford to take a chance, especially since the rate of change in consumer prices had already started to decline. So in March 1958, Jonas re-entered the market, with funds that had grown to $1,585,234. (And by December, every measure of price increases had fallen into line.)

Between March 1958 and November 1965 all four conditions remained in place, and the secular bull roared ahead. Jonas took a beating in the severe 1962 correction—that year his portfolio declined from $2,900,399 to $2,697,371—but the subsequent recovery in stocks left him far richer.** By November 1965, when he pulled out, his funds had risen to $4,350,757.

What signaled to him that the secular bull had come to an end? My second interest rate condition: Wholesale prices had risen to more than half of what bonds were

---

*Consumer prices refer to what you and I and your Aunt Mildred pay for various goods, from food to rent to the price of a movie ticket. The best-known measure of this is the Consumer Price Index (CPI), which calculates the cost of a presumably typical market basket of goods. A broader measure, but one that is harder to follow, is the GNP Price Deflator, which is what I used in my study of the ratio. Wholesale or producer prices are one step down the line. They are what businesses pay for products before they mark them up to sell to the consumer, and they are measured by the Producer Price Index (PPI).

**Followed carefully, my conditions could have provided Jonas with some advance warning of even this beating. In 1962, while the first, second, and fourth conditions remained firmly in place—strong reassurance that the long-term outlook for the secular bull remained healthy—the third condition, though not turning negative, was definitely telling investors to beware. In the twelve months leading up to the 1962 correction, the difference between long-term and short-term interest rates declined, by postwar standards, a record amount, a clear indication that the relationship between real growth and inflation, while not on the verge of turning bearish, had become at least somewhat less favorable. Remember, too, that 1962 was a period of untrammeled speculation in the technology stocks. In such a speculative climate, even a mildly less favorable economic backdrop could serve as a catalyst for a fierce shakeout.

117

yielding. This was a sign that inflation, not real growth, was becoming the driving force behind the economy, and Jonas wanted no part of it.

The next seventeen years were virtually a mirror image of the postwar period. Whereas during the earlier era my conditions were in place with just a few exceptions, during the later period they were out of place except for a few occasions. One of those occurred in January 1967, when producer prices fell below half of what bonds were yielding. Because Jonas used producer prices as his gauge of inflation, he got into the market then. And within six months consumer prices had followed suit in confirmation.

By January 1968, however, most price measures had risen to above half of bond yields, with only producer prices continuing on a remarkably well-behaved course. If Jonas had simply paid attention to this measure he would have remained in the market until mid-1969. That would have been fine, since the market remained in an upward trend during those eighteen months. However, in early 1968 Jonas noticed that the spread between long-term and short-term rates was narrowing dramatically. In fact, there were actually days and even weeks during that period in which short-term rates, Fed funds, jumped above long-term rates. Jonas sold his stocks—worth $5,118,879—in January 1968, with the Dow at 880.

Instead of getting better, things got worse. By March 1969 long-term rates fell well below short-term rates and stayed that way until August 1970. This development clearly foretold the inflationary recession that began in 1970. And it came as no surprise to Jonas that the market between early 1969 and mid-1970 was a disaster, with almost all the popular averages falling some 25%.

But by July 1970 my conditions were once again predicting better times ahead. Short-term interest rates fell below long-term rates, and producer prices marked the second consecutive month in which they increased at a rate less than half what bonds were yielding. Jonas was back in the market in August, with the Dow at 725. With help from Nixon's price controls, all four conditions remained in place for the next two years, as the market went crazy on the upside, soaring to 950. At that point Jonas realized it was time once again to shift his holdings, which had appreciated to $8,594,495, into Treasury securities. The reason: Prices—all measures—had risen above half of bond yields.

One thing may be puzzling you. I have said that my conditions predict sustainable growth and secular bull markets, and I have also said that the postwar secular bull market ended in late 1965. Yet my conditions propelled Jonas back into the market for a total of three of the seven years between the end of 1965 and late 1972. In all three the market made substantial gains, even though the overall trend for the seven years was downward. The way I see it, during those seven years there were occasional rays of hope that the economy might be getting itself back on a sustained growth path. My conditions reflected those rays of hope, as did the market's strength during those times. But the hopes were never fulfilled, my conditions would ultimately sound a warning note, and the market would retreat.

In other words, even though the postwar secular bull market essentially ended in late 1965, it is possible to view the period from then through late 1972 as the secular bull's last gasp. But in late 1972, with just one fleeting ghostly visit, the secular bull was killed off for good. During the nearly ten years between August 1972 and January 1982 my conditions were met only during one four-month period, October 1976–January 1977. Even then, most measures of price increases never fell into line. Not surprisingly, the market during those ten years was nothing to cheer about. With several ups and downs in the middle, the DJIA was 21% lower at the end of the period than at the start. Except for a brief foray into the market in late 1976, Jonas stayed in risk-free, short-term Treasury securities during the entire period. His total as of January 1982 was $18,386,015. My four conditions enabled him to realize a 183,760% gain on his original $10,000 investment over a sixty-year span. If he had simply put his money in the Dow stocks and left it there, his gain would have been only $1.3 million, almost 93% less than what he made. (See Figure 7-2.)

At this point it would be useful to summarize what I have come to think of as Jonas's Rules, the exact considerations he took into account in following the dictates of the four conditions.

## Jonas's Rules

1. The ratio of real growth to inflation should be greater than 1.
2. Inflation should be less than half of what bonds are yielding.
3. Long-term interest rates should be above short-term rates.

120

**FIGURE 7-2**

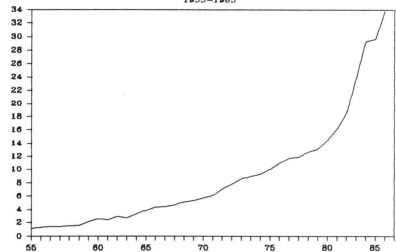

Jonas's Portfolio
1955–1985

4. Money supply growth must be in an uptrend according to the Rule of 3s.

## Refinements

1. If the ratio is below 1 because growth is negative, and all other rules are satisfied, you can invest, since a growing money supply implies that growth will soon turn positive.

2. If the second condition is not met but all others are, and if in addition money supply growth remains below real growth, you can invest, since the latter circumstance implies inflation isn't a major long-term problem. (One example

of how Jonas applied this rule was during the Korean War, when extraordinary conditions created a bulge in prices that was not confirmed by a sharply accelerating money supply.)

3. In applying the second condition, producer prices should be the most important gauge. Specifically, use a five-month average of the year-over-year rate of change in the Producer Price Index. The condition turns from negative to positive if the PPI satisfies our criterion—which is to say, if the five-month average of the PPI is below half of what bonds are yielding and if the most recent monthly figure is also below this level—*and* if consumer price increases (again use a five-month average) are declining.*

4. In applying the third condition, Jonas used a six-month average of the ratio of long-term to short-term rates.** In post–World War II history, long-term yields were measured by AAA corporate bonds, while Fed funds defined short-term rates. (Except for 1929, prior to 1949 this condition was not a factor.)

5. When Jonas was out of stocks he had two choices. He could invest in bonds—with the potential for capital gains as well as the risk of capital losses—or he could park his money in short-term instruments such as T-bills. When Condition No. 3 was positive, Jonas opted for bonds; when it was negative he went for risk-free T-bills.

---

*Jonas used five-month averages, but actually this is somewhat arbitrary. If you were to use a shorter (one-to-four month) or longer (six-to-twelve month) average it would have very little impact on the results.

**Again, a shorter or longer average would have worked just about as well.

\*     \*     \*

Jonas's rules and refinements had served him well. They got him into the market for the bulk of the two and a half secular bull markets and at a few other moments besides, when the bull, though not secular, was nonetheless kicking up his heels. They kept Jonas out of the market during nearly all periods of downturn. (See Figure 7-3.)

**FIGURE 7-3**

## JONAS'S PORTFOLIO
## 1922–1985

| Date | Dow | Total Return | Jonas's Strategy | Jonas's Portfolio |
|------|-----|--------------|------------------|-------------------|
| Feb 1922 | 89.1 | 14.9 | Stocks | $10,000 |
| Jan 1923 | 98.8 | 1.7 | Stocks | 11,489 |
| Jan 1924 | 95.7 | 32.0 | Stocks | 11,684 |
| Jan 1925 | 121.3 | 34.8 | Stocks | 15,423 |
| Jan 1926 | 158.5 | 1.5 | Stocks | 20,791 |
| Jan 1927 | 155.2 | 34.6 | Stocks | 21,102 |
| Jan 1928 | 203.4 | 55.2 | Stocks | 28,404 |
| Jan 1929 | 307.0 | 10.5 | Stocks | 44,083 |
| May 1929 | 333.8 | 3.2 | Income | 48,703 |
| Oct 1929 | 239.0 | 21.1 | Stocks | 50,261 |
| Feb 1930 | 286.1 | 4.0 | Income | 60,841 |
| Jan 1931 | | 1.0 | Income | 63,275 |
| Jan 1932 | | 19.0 | Income | 63,908 |
| Jan 1933 | | 13.0 | Income | 76,050 |
| Oct 1933 | 98.1 | 3.3 | Stocks | 85,937 |
| Jan 1934 | 100.4 | 7.9 | Stocks | 88,772 |

| Date | Dow | Total Return | Jonas's Strategy | Jonas's Portfolio |
|------|-----|--------------|------------------|-------------------|
| Jan 1935 | 104.5 | 42.0 | Stocks | 95,786 |
| Jan 1936 | 144.1 | 36.0 | Stocks | 136,015 |
| Jan 1937 | 187.0 | 6.1 | Income | 184,981 |
| Jan 1938 | | 6.0 | Income | 196,265 |
| Sep 1938 | 135.5 | 14.5 | Stocks | 208,041 |
| Jan 1940 | 148.0 | 2.8 | Income | 238,207 |
| Jan 1941 | | 2.8 | Income | 244,876 |
| Jan 1942 | | 2.8 | Income | 251,733 |
| Jan 1943 | | 6.3 | Income | 258,781 |
| Jan 1944 | | 2.7 | Income | 275,085 |
| Jan 1945 | | 9.5 | Income | 282,512 |
| Jan 1946 | | 4.0 | Income | 309,351 |
| Jan 1947 | | 1.0 | Income | 321,725 |
| Jan 1948 | | 6.3 | Income | 324,942 |
| Jan 1949 | | 2.7 | Income | 345,413 |
| Aug 1949 | 178.7 | 17.0 | Stocks | 354,739 |
| Jan 1950 | 198.9 | 27.0 | Stocks | 415,045 |
| Jan 1951 | 239.9 | 18.5 | Stocks | 527,107 |
| Jan 1952 | 269.9 | 14.0 | Stocks | 624,622 |
| Jan 1953 | 292.1 | 2.0 | Stocks | 712,069 |
| Jan 1954 | 282.9 | 50.0 | Stocks | 726,311 |
| Jan 1955 | 408.9 | 23.5 | Stocks | 1,089,466 |
| Jan 1956 | 485.8 | 8.5 | Stocks | 1,345,490 |
| Apr 1956 | 518.0 | 1.2 | Income | 1,459,857 |
| Jan 1957 | | 5.3 | Income | 1,477,375 |
| Jan 1958 | | 1.9 | Income | 1,555,676 |
| Mar 1958 | 446.8 | 35.5 | Stocks | 1,585,234 |
| Jan 1959 | 587.6 | 18.5 | Stocks | 2,147,992 |
| Jan 1960 | 679.1 | −6.6 | Stocks | 2,545,371 |
| Jan 1961 | 610.3 | 22.0 | Stocks | 2,377,376 |

| Date | Dow | Total Return | Jonas's Strategy | Jonas's Portfolio |
|------|-----|--------------|------------------|-------------------|
| Jan 1962 | 724.7 | −7.0 | Stocks | 2,900,399 |
| Jan 1963 | 646.8 | 22.0 | Stocks | 2,697,371 |
| Jan 1964 | 766.1 | 17.0 | Stocks | 3,290,793 |
| Jan 1965 | 869.8 | 13.0 | Stocks | 3,850,228 |
| Nov 1965 | 959.9 | 1.0 | Income | 4,350,757 |
| Jan 1966 | | 5.9 | Income | 4,394,265 |
| Jan 1967 | 825.0 | 10.0 | Stocks | 4,653,527 |
| Jan 1968 | 880.0 | 4.3 | Income | 5,118,879 |
| Jan 1969 | | 6.7 | Income | 5,338,991 |
| Jan 1970 | | 7.0 | Income | 5,696,703 |
| Aug 1970 | 725.0 | 16.0 | Stocks | 6,095,473 |
| Jan 1971 | 830.6 | 10.5 | Stocks | 7,070,748 |
| Jan 1972 | 889.3 | 10.0 | Stocks | 7,813,177 |
| Aug 1972 | 950.5 | 5.0 | Income | 8,594,495 |
| Jan 1973 | | 3.0 | Income | 9,024,219 |
| Jan 1974 | | 7.9 | Income | 9,294,946 |
| Jan 1975 | | 8.8 | Income | 10,029,247 |
| Jan 1976 | | 7.0 | Income | 10,911,820 |
| Sep 1976 | 980.0 | 1.4 | Stocks | 11,675,648 |
| Jan 1977 | 980.0 | 7.0 | Income | 11,839,107 |
| Jan 1978 | | 3.6 | Income | 12,667,844 |
| Jan 1979 | | 10.0 | Income | 13,123,887 |
| Jan 1980 | | 11.6 | Income | 14,441,525 |
| Jan 1981 | | 14.1 | Income | 16,118,186 |
| Jan 1982 | 845.0 | 29.2 | Stocks | 18,386,015 |
| Jan 1983 | 1040.0 | 23.5 | Stocks | 23,754,731 |
| Jan 1984 | 1240.0 | 1.0 | Stocks | 29,337,093 |
| Jan 1985 | 1190.0 | 14.0 | Stocks | 29,630,464 |
| Jun 1985 | 1330.0 | | Stocks | 33,778,728 |

By 1982, Jonas had developed an almost superstitious attachment to the system entrusted to him. Jonas felt that life had been good to him: a long and generally happy marriage, four children, six grandchildren, a successful law practice. In his conscious mind he knew that all this had little to do with the stock market. But somewhere in his subconscious he connected his general good fortune with his willingness over the years to stick to a rigorous investment system, never trying to second-guess it to wring out an extra dollar of profit. Jonas saw no reason to change his approach now, and when in 1982 my conditions told him that it was time to get back in the market, Jonas didn't hesitate; he dived back in.

# 8

# THE BIRTH OF THE SECULAR BULL

What had Jonas seen, at the age of eighty-two, when most men would be content to live off the considerable income generated by an $18 million fortune, that made him call his broker and enter the turbulent world of stocks once again?

The first piece of evidence came toward the end of 1981. Condition No. 2—long-term interest rates more than twice inflation—gave the initial signal. In November, for the first time since 1976, long-term bond yields, as measured both on a monthly basis and on the basis of a five-month moving average, exceeded inflation, as measured by the Producer Price Index.

Meanwhile, Condition No. 4, growth in the money supply, had been consistently positive even during the 1970s and early 1980s.

The event that truly propelled Jonas back into the market occurred in January 1982, when long-term rates moved above short-term rates—the crucial Condition No. 3 was back on the job. It was the first time that

Conditions No. 2 and 3 had been in place simultaneously in six years.

With Conditions No. 2 through 4 in place, Jonas knew that it was just a matter of time before No. 1 also operated.* But he knew, too, that if he waited for this final piece of evidence, he would miss the first part of the big bull move that he was confident was just around the corner. Sometime in January Jonas was on the phone with his very pleased broker, telling him he was getting back into the market.

Yes, Jonas was a bit early—around seven months, to be precise. But he had cultivated a long-term perspective about the market and knew that what counts is being vindicated in the end—as he was sure he would be.** The market's explosive rally in August, and the follow-through in subsequent months, came as no surprise to him.

It did, however, catch the majority of market pros off guard. As in the periods before the secular bull markets of the 1920s and 1949–1965, the general mood on Wall Street in the days before the August rally was bleak. The rampant pessimism was well caught in an article that, with impeccable timing, appeared in the business section of *The New York Times* on Sunday, August 15. The headline proclaimed, "Dark Days on Wall Street"; underneath was a large graph whose thick, dark, jaggedly descending line starkly portrayed the relentless decline of the Dow since April 1981. The gist of the

---

*The ratio of real growth to inflation fell into place during the first or second quarter of 1983, depending upon which measure of inflation you use. In the first quarter, the Gross National Product grew by 3.3%, as compared with a rise in producer prices of less than 1%. If you go by the GNP Price Deflator, however, the ratio did not rise above 1 until the second quarter.
**As of June 1985 his portfolio had risen to over $33 million.

article was that nearly everyone on Wall Street was anticipating at least one more cataclysmic move down, an enormous selling spree that would send the DJIA to lows not seen in many a year. After that, anything was possible. Said one money manager, who understandably wished to remain anonymous: "Nobody can tell if we're starting a depression or ending one. The market is one giant gamble."

Business leaders, the heads of the country's top corporations, also saw very little light ahead. In May, for the semiannual conference of the Business Council, executives gathered in the lush surroundings of the old-fashioned resort hotel, the Homestead, in Hot Springs, Virginia. For a group that generally serves as cheerleaders for the economy, they were unusually pessimistic, unwilling to forecast economic growth ahead.

The chain of events in 1982, then, is familiar: a relentlessly falling market, a depressed economy, and predictions of far worse to come, followed by a suddenly explosive market and, shortly afterward, an economic recovery far stronger than anyone had anticipated. And, under the surface, *my four conditions shifting into gear, telling those who can read their signals that a fundamental change had taken place in the economy, a sea change that meant that this time around, the good times will not be inevitably followed by the bad, at least not for many many years.*

The fact that the four conditions were all in place by early 1983 and have remained there ever since tells us that the odds overwhelmingly favor our having entered a sustained-growth economy and a secular bull market. But I wanted to go a little further—to see if I could discover *why* the conditions re-emerged when they did.

129

For if we can answer that, we will be able to know with greater certainty whether the conditions can be relied on to remain in place for many years to come or whether, as occasionally happened in the late 1960s and early 1970s, they reflect rays of hope that will prove ephemeral.

The obvious and immediate answer, of course, is that the conditions fell into place in 1982 because that was when, after years of plaguing American life, inflation had finally been licked. (See Figure 8-1.) In the early 1960s, as the second secular bull market was enjoying its twilight years, inflation as measured by the Consumer Price Index was always well below 2%. In 1966, however, there was a sharp spike upward to 2.9%; by 1968 prices were rising by 4.2% a year, and in 1970 the figure had risen to 5.9%. But the following decade was when inflation, with an assist from OPEC and a declining dollar, really began to get scary. After coming down a bit, prices by 1974 were rising at a steamy 11.0% a year; they cooled off only to rise at a 15% annual rate in early 1980.

For a while it looked as if the U.S. might be headed for the hyperinflation of countries like Israel or Argentina. It is easy to forget just how alarming those days were. I recall talking to the wife of an attorney at a dinner party in the late 1970s who was telling me that every week she would go out to buy cat food and find that the price of a box of Tender Vittles had risen by another 10 cents or so. This woman wasn't really worried about keeping her cat fed. But she was deeply afraid that in a few years, when her husband was due to retire, his pension would no longer be sufficient to enable them to live in their accustomed style. In those days, inflation was not just a minor irritation, it was a gnawing anxiety that was eating away at the insides of many of us.

## FIGURE 8-1

# Inflation: 1956 – 1984*

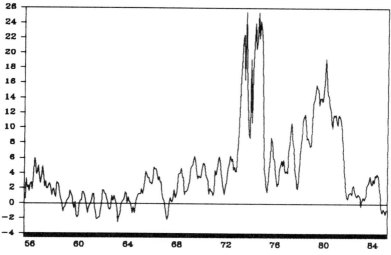

*Rate of change in producer prices.

By the end of 1984, however, inflation as measured by wholesale prices was advancing by a mere 1% a year. Many people give the credit to Paul A. Volcker, who became chairman of the Federal Reserve in August 1979. Volcker is, by all accounts, a remarkable man who combines abundant, apparently innate political gifts with a disdain for conventional politics. It is clear that he came to Washington determined to squeeze inflation out of the system, and to do so in such an unmistakably firm manner as to inspire long-lasting confidence in the financial markets.

The steps taken by the Fed under Volcker's direction have been frequently recounted—starting with his decision to stop focusing on direct control of interest rates and instead to concentrate on slowing the growth of the money supply—and it isn't necessary to detail them here. Suffice it to say that Volcker demonstrated in instance after instance that he was willing to risk the wrath of the White House (under both Carter and Reagan) and to lead the country into severe recession to bring inflation under control. It was tricky. Tighter money means less inflation, but it also means higher interest rates, which, by making money more expensive, can stifle growth and lead to recession. On the other hand, there was the possibility that an easier-money policy would also result in higher interest rates by raising fears that inflation might erupt once again. In other words, for a while Volcker had to endure a damned-if-you-do-damned-if-you-don't situation until he had finally established enough credibility as an inflation-fighter that when he did ease, people would believe that it was because there was room to ease and not because he was caving in to political pressure. That he was able to pull this off is an enormous tribute to his tenacity and talent.

But while Volcker achieved near-saint status on Wall Street, my four conditions do not owe their re-emergence to him alone. Nor are they ultimately indebted to the supply-side policies of President Reagan, as some might argue. Yes, the faith that Volcker inspired in the financial markets in this country and abroad has been significant, and yes, Reagan embodies a pro-business attitude that has had a positive impact on the investment decisions of some companies. But the actions of one or two individuals are insufficient to account for such a broad, basic change as the shift from a cyclical economy to one on a secular growth path.

Other, deeper changes were taking place below the surface, digging up the soil of American life and working to let some fresh air in. These changes, these long-term trends, were slowly laying a solid groundwork for continued low inflation, sustained growth—and a secular bull market. And this is a good thing. For if the taming of inflation resulted solely from the decisions of one or two people in power, then a changing of the guard at the White House or the Fed could send inflation soaring again. However, because I am skeptical of the hero theory of history, preferring to look for underlying causes, I don't see any danger of that happening.

I have identified four deep-rooted, ongoing trends that I think are largely responsible for the emergence of our conditions in 1982—for the curbing of inflation without sacrificing growth. They are: *changing demographics, the rise in entrepreneurship, deregulation,* and *the dawning of the information age.* All four had their genesis many years ago, but have only relatively recently begun to bear fruit in the form of low inflation and high real growth. Only one, deregulation, can be considered to result primarily from changes in government policy, and it is worth noting that the real push for deregulation came during the administration of Jimmy Carter, a Democrat, and that the move toward less regulation has widespread bipartisan acceptance. I think each of these trends has an irreversible momentum for now, meaning that my conditions are in no danger of being dislodged anytime soon. Let's look at these trends.

133

# Changing Demographics

Many of you in your thirties and forties probably still get a tight feeling in your stomach when you think back to the days when you were applying to college. What were the odds that you would get into the school of your choice, or even your second or third choice? One in seven, one in ten? Everybody knew that competition for places was fierce and that even top students had no guarantee of ending up where they wanted.

And you undoubtedly knew the reason, too: You were a member of the infamous baby boom generation. For your entire life, you would be part of a bulge in the population, doomed to move through life uncomfortably squeezed against your fellow travelers, a passenger on a plane with too few seats, maneuvering to catch the eye of an overworked stewardess and grab a dinner tray before there was none left.

After school comes the real world and the need to find a job. Since 1966, when the first of the baby boomers came of age, growth in the labor force began steadily accelerating. This trend was helped along by affirmative action programs and by the growing number of women seeking to enter the work force. From the mid-1960s to 1980, the growth rate of the labor force nearly doubled, from about 1.5% a year to 3%.

But in the early 1980s something very significant happened, as evidenced by Figure 8-2. *The growth of the labor force started to slow down.* For one thing, the last of the baby boomers had been absorbed into the workplace. Also, because so many women had already gotten jobs outside the home, the female participation rate

134

began to level off. As a result, the labor force once again began growing by about 1.5%. The heady days of rapid work-force growth should remain behind us through at least the rest of the century.

FIGURE 8-2

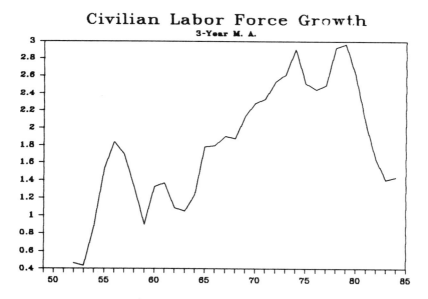

## Civilian Labor Force Growth
### 3-Year M. A.

A more slowly growing labor force is bullish for several reasons:

*First,* when a lot of people are seeking jobs, the government is under pressure to promote overly stimulative policies to prevent unemployment from reaching unacceptable levels. Just consider the fact that today, if the labor force were growing 1 percentage point faster than it is, the unemployment rate would be 1 percentage point higher. It is easy to see why, under such circumstances, unemployment would soon become such a headache that the government would be willing to reach for almost any pill to make it go away. But in this case the remedy—pumping money into the system in the hope of causing the economy to spurt forward and provide more and more jobs as it goes—has some unpleasant aftereffects. Such growth tends to be faster than the economy can handle, and the ultimate result is rising inflation.

*Second,* a rapidly growing labor force encourages business to devote more resources to labor than to capital. It becomes easier and cheaper to hire more workers than to invest in capital improvements. During the 1960s and 1970s, moreover, this imbalance was accentuated by the requirements of government-mandated affirmative action programs designed to bring women, blacks, and Hispanics into the workplace in greater numbers. Whatever the social and moral value of such programs, they were costly to employers, both because of the greatly increased paperwork associated with hiring and, more important, because overall the work force became less skilled and therefore less productive. Among the most reliable measures of overall skills are scores on the Scholastic Aptitude Tests (SATs) given to high school seniors who plan to go on to college. Starting in the mid-1960s there was a sharp drop in SAT scores. In 1965 math plus verbal scores averaged 980. By 1980 and 1981 they had fallen to 890. The upshot of all these trends was that employee compensation as a percentage of the national income leaped upward in the mid-1960s, from under 70% to over 75%, and remained high until the early 1980s. (See Figure 8-3.)

Affirmative action programs are still with us, of

136

FIGURE 8-3

## Math + Verbal SAT Scores

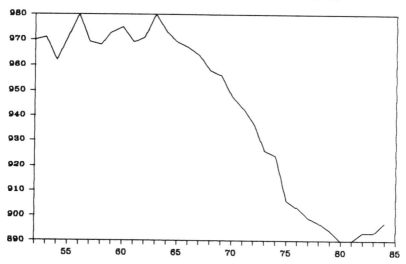

course, but they are less of a factor. One reason is the leveling off in the number of women seeking jobs. Equally significant, the entire work force is becoming more skilled. In 1982, for the first time in almost a generation, SAT scores turned up. According to the Educational Testing Service, which administers the SATs, this was largely attributable to better scores by women and minorities. The implication is that the inflationary impact of affirmative action programs is likely to lessen as the "skill spread" among various population groups narrows. Also contributing to the brighter picture is that older workers, those hired in the 1960s and 1970s, are now more seasoned.

It all adds up to a strong case for continued gains in

137

productivity, continued moderation in unit labor costs, and a decreasing share of GNP devoted to employee compensation. These concomitants of changing demographics are a major reason why the third year of the economic recovery that began in 1982 resembles, in terms of inflation, nothing that we have seen in the mid-1960s to 1980. And they are a major reason for believing that the downtrend in inflation is a secular shift.

## The Rise in Entrepreneurship

The entrepreneurial spirit seems to erupt in the U.S. in waves, sweeping over the country for a time and then subsiding a bit. There are various ways to measure its waxing and waning. The statistical series with the longest history is the number of new concerns formed each year, for which there is data going back more than one hundred years. Figure 8-4 depicts the number of new concerns going back as far as 1870.

There is another way to measure entrepreneurship, and that is to see where new jobs are coming from. In the 1950s and 1960s, large corporations provided the bulk of new jobs. But in 1970 that began to change. In the ensuing decade employment in the U.S. jumped by about 20 million, and Fortune 500 companies were responsible for very little of this growth: Nearly all of these new jobs were generated by relatively small start-up businesses. This trend became even more pronounced during the turbulent years from 1980 to 1983. As the economy went through two recessions, Fortune 500 companies lost about 3 million jobs, while companies less than ten years old added some 750,000 jobs.

138

## FIGURE 8-4

### New Concerns (in millions)

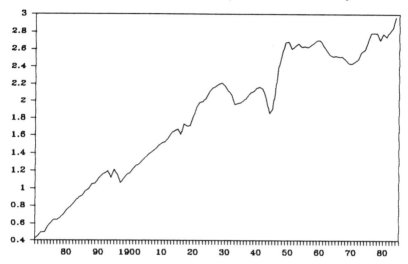

Starting in the early 1970s, small businesses headed by entrepreneurs have become the engine of economic growth.

The ability of the economy to generate a steady stream of new businesses is extremely bullish. Small businesses, because they are starting from a more limited base, can sustain fast growth for long periods. Moreover, they have been responsible for nearly every major industrial innovation in our history. Examples from the present era abound, from personal computers to warehousing to biotechnology.

An influx of aggressive, innovative young companies headed by entrepreneurs stimulates the entire economy. As happened with personal computers, it can result in the formation of entire new industries that in turn necessitate the creation of other brand-new industries to service them. The start-ups also stimulate older, more established companies to compete more vigorously. For example, after allowing itself to be beaten to the punch by Apple, IBM eventually introduced its own personal computer, the PC. It is this kind of interaction that makes for a growing, exciting economy.

Is it possible to quantify the entrepreneurial spirit in relation to secular bull markets? Yes. Let's return to the statistical series of new concerns formed each year. Only this time turn to Figure 8-5, "New Business Concerns: 10-Year Rate of Change," and look at it in relation to Figure 8-6, "S&P 400 10-Year Rate of Change."

*It turns out that in all cases a peak in the formation of new concerns preceded an important stock market peak.* In some cases, it was by as few as three years, as in the late 1920s. Other times, as with the post–World War II bull market, it was by as much as a decade. But in all cases a major bull trend did not end until after a peak in entrepreneurial activity. Conversely, a trough in this series preceded all major market troughs. Again, there were variable time lags, but the relationship is real and undeniable.

We are, in other words, looking at a genuine secular lead indicator. And its implications for the present are extremely bullish. The number of new concerns reached a trough in 1970, just four years before a trough in secondary stocks in 1974 and twelve years prior to the market's major secular bottom in August 1982. In 1984 the number of new concerns was at a new high and still rising, which is, of course, consistent with our observations about the source of new jobs since 1970. Given the record of this indicator in the past, *the message is that even if the growth in new concerns were to end now—which it shows no signs of doing—we would still be at least three years away from a major market top. And assuming that the growth in new concerns continues, we could be ten, fifteen, or twenty years from a major top.*

FIGURE 8-5

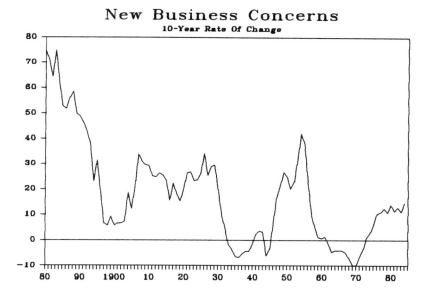

## New Business Concerns
10-Year Rate Of Change

## Deregulation

Over the past decade and a half, deregulation has altered the rules of major areas of American industry—in particular, telecommunications, transportation, and financial services. The reins have been loosened, and

141

while some companies and individuals have gotten hurt in the subsequent free-for-all, the overall result has been increased productivity, more innovation, and lower inflation.

FIGURE 8-6

## S&P 400 10-Year Rate Of Change

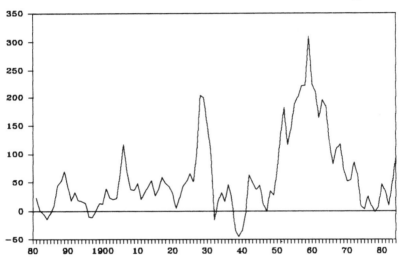

An article in *Business Week* in late 1983 estimated that in the seven preceding years, as a result of deregulation, long-distance airline fares, adjusted for inflation, had declined by nearly 50%. Trucking rates were down 30% over three years, while the cost of buying a standard telephone had fallen by one-third in one year. In the financial services area, the cost to a customer of buying or selling stock had declined by 60%.

Originally government regulation of industry, which

142

received its big thrust in the New Deal, was intended to protect the ordinary consumer, the little guy, against the greedy instincts of big companies with monopolistic aspirations. As time went on, however, it became increasingly clear that in general regulation was simply safeguarding the position of a few large, established companies. Within the regulated industries there was no incentive to innovate, to keep costs down, or to strive to meet the needs of a captive customer base. Consumers as a group, and the economy as a whole, were the losers. As this became evident, deregulation, once something that only die-hard conservatives dared suggest, became a cause that politicians of all stripes could embrace.

Deregulation began hesitantly in the late 1960s and gradually gathered momentum, with Congress and various agencies all playing a role. The first milestone was the 1968 decision by the Supreme Court to let non-AT&T equipment be connected to the AT&T system. A year later the Federal Communications Commission gave MCI the right to plug its long-distance lines into local phone systems. In 1970 the Federal Reserve Board freed interest rates on certain categories of bank deposits. In 1974 the Justice Department brought its historic antitrust suit against AT&T, which would result in the breakup of Ma Bell in January 1984. In 1975 the Securities and Exchange Commission ordered brokers to stop fixing commissions on stock transactions. In 1978 Congress deregulated the airlines. In 1980 the Fed allowed banks to pay interest on checking accounts. That same year Congress deregulated trucking and railroads; intercity bus service was next, in 1982.

The airlines industry offers one of the clearest examples of the impact and benefits of deregulation. In just a few years, the industry went through a complete restructuring. New carriers, such as Midway, People Express, and New York Air, began operations, and because of their more intensive use of planes and their willingness to rely on less congested airports and to employ nonunion labor, they started with cost levels estimated at 25% to 30% below those of their bigger rivals. As a result, older airlines had to bargain hard to get more productivity from their employees. The upshot was that for these big "trunk" airlines, output per employee was 27% higher in 1979–1980 than in 1973–1975. In other areas of transportation, and in the other industries that have been recently deregulated, the effects have been similar.

In sum, deregulation has energized major sectors of American industry, forcing them to wake up, look around, and start to compete. It has helped keep wage increases down, a major factor in keeping inflation well-behaved. Equally important to the secular bull, deregulation has led to the freer and more efficient movement of goods, information, and capital essential to continued economic growth.

## The Dawning of the Information Age

The U.S. economy can be divided into two broad sectors: information—which is often referred to as services—and goods. The former includes areas such as retailing, finance, real estate, trade, transportation, communications, and public utilities. The latter consists of manufacturing, mining, and construction.

(Farming is generally considered apart from both goods and services.)

Several significant things have been happening over the past few decades with respect to this distinction. They can be summarized as: growth of the information sector relative to the goods sector, growth in the relative numbers of information workers in both sectors, and the increasing capitalization of the information sector.

### 1. GROWTH OF THE INFORMATION SECTOR

In the mid-1960s the information sector began to grow while the goods sector began to shrink. Between 1966 and 1985 the share of total economic output contributed by the information sector climbed from 55% to an estimated 67%. The share contributed by goods dropped from 45% to 33%.

### 2. GROWTH IN INFORMATION WORKERS

Both sectors employ both information and goods workers. Within the information sector itself, information workers are managers, scientists, computer programmers, and so on; goods or production workers are maintenance people, building-support staff, printers, transportation operators, etc.

The goods sector also needs information workers— managers and their support staff. Production workers are everyone else, from machine operators to assembly-line workers.

Not surprisingly, the information sector employs more information workers than it does goods workers, while the reverse is true for the goods sector. But what is significant is that information workers are becoming an increasingly large portion of both sectors, as you can see from Figure 8-7.

145

FIGURE 8-7

## EMPLOYMENT COMPOSITION

|  | Average 1962–72 | | 1983 | |
|  | Information Workers | Production Workers | Information Workers | Production Workers |
| --- | --- | --- | --- | --- |
| Information Sector | 62.3% | 37.7% | 65.7% | 34.3% |
| Goods Sector | 28.7 | 71.3 | 33.6 | 66.4 |
| Total Nonfarm Work Force | 49.2 | 50.8 | 56.2 | 43.8 |

*Source:* Morgan Stanley.

3. GROWTH IN CAPITAL EXPENDITURES DEVOTED TO HIGH-TECH INVESTMENT

Since 1965 the portion of capital outlays devoted to high technologies—computers, communications equipment, instruments, and measuring devices—has jumped from 12% to an estimated 35% or more in 1985. Conversely, the portion of capital outlays devoted to basic industrial investment—heavy machinery, industrial buildings, etc.—has fallen over the same period from over 25% to an estimated 12% or so. (Other investment categories such as farm equipment, commercial buildings, energy conservation, and transportation equipment account for the remainder.)

*What is particularly significant is that the disparity between the investment rates in high-tech and basic industry has been far greater than the disparity between the growth rates of information workers and production workers.* In fact, in 1984, for the first time ever, the capital stock available to the information worker exceeded the capital stock available to the production worker. Information workers, rather than remaining the poor cousins of the factory worker, are getting more "stuff"—computers, telephones, and the like—with which to ply their trade. The information worker is finally coming into his or her own.

These statistics tell two things. First, they help explain why productivity growth lagged during the 1970s and early 1980s: During those years the fastest-growing segment of the economy, the information sector, was suffering from a relative dearth of capital. Second, they point to a revival of productivity growth in the years ahead now that this has been remedied. This is a powerfully bullish implication.

The other bullish conclusion is that the growing importance of information in our economy has made us less dependent on basic commodities. In the relatively recent past, strong economic growth went hand in hand with inflation in the prices of basic commodities such as metals, coffee, sugar, and various raw materials. But today, because growth is being generated more and more by users of information rather than by users of commodities, strong growth does not imply commodity inflation. Figure 8-8 proves the point. It measures the inflation rate at the most basic level—crude materials. Despite OPEC, there has been almost no inflation at this most basic level. The results are even more striking than Figure 8-8 shows. The index measuring crude material inflation is today 4.1% lower than it was in mid-1981. Over the past three and a half years we have experienced *deflation* at this most basic level.

Such statistics make it possible to conclude that this is the first economic cycle in modern times in which a

147

FIGURE 8-8

## Crude Material Inflation Rate

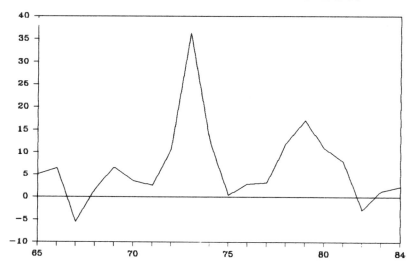

slump in basic commodity prices has not triggered a deep recession. The reason is the emergence of the information age. The most basic implication is that our economy is no longer hostage to commodity shortages. *The engine of the inflation of the 1970s is in a secular stall.*

Perhaps an even more direct effect of the technological endowment of the information sector is the way that inflation within that sector has behaved recently (Figure 8-9). Two observations are in order. First, the percentage-point drop in the inflation rate in this sector, which accounts for nearly 75% of all payroll jobs, has been greater than in other sectors. Second, and equally striking, is how inflation in this sector behaved in the current cycle as opposed to the mid-1970s. In the earlier period the drop-off was extremely mild:

148

less than 2 percentage points between the peak in 1975 and the trough in 1977. In the current cycle there has been a drop of some 10 percentage points.

**FIGURE 8-9**

## Services Inflation Rate

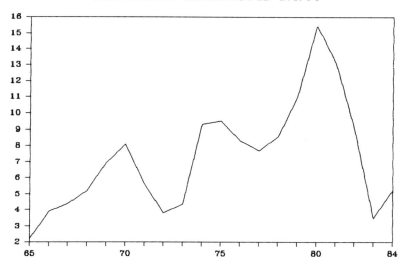

Now, you could reply that the behavior of inflation in the information sector results in part from the behavior of inflation in basic commodities. After all, more than one-third of all workers in the information sector are production workers. But this argument doesn't hold water. The reason is that the fall in commodity inflation in the 1970s, while not as long-lasting, was actually deeper than in the current cycle—it went from more than 35% in 1973 to below ½% in 1975. This time around, the drop was far smaller, from 17% in 1979 to

149

roughly 0 over the 1982–1985 period, while the drop in inflation in the service sector was far greater than in the earlier period. The unavoidable conclusion is that the growing amount of capital available to information workers is what accounts for the difference.

So there you have the four basic trends. Together they are operating to stimulate real growth while keeping inflation moderate. Their existence should keep my four conditions moored securely in place—giving confidence that the bull market that began in August 1982 is indeed the real thing—the secular bull himself.

# 9

# GETTING TO THE TOP

Now we get to the fun part: contemplating just what lies ahead. How high will stocks ultimately go, and how will they get there? As of mid-1985 the DJIA has advanced from its low of 780 to the 1300 area, a gain of about 67%. Not bad—but still rather restrained when compared with the 500% rise in the 1920s and the 1949–1965 period. If we are truly in a secular bull market, we are still in a relatively young one. What size will the bull eventually attain? How high is high?

Let me state my conclusion right up front. I believe that before this bull market subsides, sometime in the early 1990s, the DJIA will have crossed the 4000 mark and may be as high as 4500. This may sound improbably high. So, once, did 1000. And of course there is no guarantee that I'm right. But there are solid reasons for thinking that I am—reasons derived by returning, once again, to the two secular bull markets of the past.

Basically, I discovered that secular bull markets go through three distinct stages. In each stage, different

151

factors are responsible for pushing the bull to ever higher levels. In the first and third stages, *fundamental factors*—in the form of earnings growth—are crucial. By contrast, during the long middle stage, earnings growth takes a back seat. In that second stage the market is propelled almost exclusively by *psychological factors*—in the form of increasing valuations.

Understanding these stages is the key to understanding how high the secular bull can go. But first let's explore the notion of fundamental and psychological factors in a little more detail.

Consider the following equation: $P = (P/E) \times E$, where P stands for the price of a stock, E for earnings, and P/E for the price/earnings ratio.

Note that there is nothing obscure or difficult about this formula. It is about as simple as saying $2 \times 2 = 4$; in fact, it is precisely as simple as asserting that $4 = 4/2 \times 2$. But simple as it is, it is exceedingly useful in helping to explain exactly what moves the price of a stock, which in turn lets us make a sensible projection as to how high the current market can go.

Basically, the right-hand side of the equation has two different kinds of components. The first term on the right-hand side—the P/E ratio—is what I call the *valuation component*. The second term on the right-hand side—earnings—I call the *fundamental component*.

The latter is a question of hard fact. It is a number that can be found by scanning a company's balance sheet and looking for the entry on earnings (per share). At any moment in time it is a given.

The valuation component, however, is of a different character. It has to do with psychology, not hard numbers. Its level at any one time stems from investors' perceptions about the potential worth of a company. I touched on this earlier in discussing the concept of premiums and discounts to book. Whether a company sells at 10 times earnings or 50 times earnings, or below or above book value, relates to what investors expect of the company in terms of future growth. And expectations are a function of psychology.

Together the two components determine the price of a stock. Valuation times fundamentals—psychology times the balance sheet—is what accounts for a stock's price at any time. At some moments, though, the valuation component is more significant, while at other times the fundamental factor plays the more important role. This is where the three stages come in.

## Stage 1:
## Recovery from Recession

During the first stage of each of the two secular bull markets of the past—lasting one to two years—the fundamental component was key. Corporate earnings growth during those years was extremely rapid. In 1922 the earnings of DJIA companies spurted a spectacular 334%, from $2.10 a share to $9.11 a share. In 1950 Dow profits rose from $23.54 a share to $30.70 a share.

The market responded to this growth by making substantial gains of its own. Between 1921 and 1923 the DJIA gained 62%, while from 1949 to 1950 it climbed 46%. And there is no doubt at all that during those years the rise in stocks stemmed entirely from the growth in corporate profits. P/E's actually *fell*—growth was there but investors, far from being willing to award

153

such growth higher capitalizations, were actually becoming warier about the prospects for stocks. Thus, in 1922 Dow companies had an average P/E of only a little more than 10, compared with 13 in 1920 and 1921. Similarly, in 1950 the capitalization of Dow companies fell from 7.7 to 7.0. In the initial stage of each secular bull market the psychological component was actually a drag on stock prices.

This is not hard to explain. The exceedingly rapid profit growth during those years was possible because in both cases the economy was emerging from a severe recession, and profits were being compared to recessionary levels. During recessions, companies are unable to cut costs enough to compensate for the slowdown in sales. When sales start to recover at the beginning of an expansion, the effect is quite different. The added revenues do not necessitate a commensurate rise in costs, since there is generally no need to add extra plant or equipment to meet the increased demand. The result is that a large proportion of the added revenues flows directly to the bottom line, and profits rise dramatically. But investors tend to distrust what they see. Having gotten used to bad times, investors are cynical, unable to believe that good fortune might last.

It's like a baseball team. If a team has been losing for several years and then one season gets off to a fast start, no one is likely right off to bet the house on its winning the pennant. You'd want to wait and see more. But if the team continues to win game after game, and what's more, it dawns on you that its success can be attributed largely to a new manager and some shrewd trades at the start of the year—to a change in the *fundamental* underpinnings—then, to paraphrase Tug McGraw, you might start to believe. The growing willingness of investors to believe is what leads to the secular bull's second stage.

The secular bull market of the 1980s has been following the same pattern. Between 1982 and 1984 earnings of Dow companies rose a hefty 84%, from $62 to $114, as the economy emerged from deep recession. P/E's fell, from 14 to 11. And the market soared 66%, to the 1300 level. The market in those two years sailed through Stage 1 in classic form.

# Stage 2:
# The Era of Psychology

During the long second stage of secular bull markets—which is when the market makes the bulk of its gains—everything is reversed. Earnings growth slows down to where it is almost negligible, and steadily expanding P/E's take over as the propelling force behind the rise in stocks. The valuation, or *psychological,* factor becomes key.

Between 1922 and 1927 there was virtually no profit growth for the Dow companies. In fact, like a mirror image of the first stage, the fundamental component was actually a negative contributor. During those years Dow earnings, believe it or not, *declined* from $9.11 a share to $8.72 a share. Yet the Dow rose from a low of 78 in 1922 to a high of 202 in 1927, a 159% gain.

As for the second secular bull market, from 1950 to 1961 Dow earnings rose a scant 3.9%, from $30.70 a share to $31.91. That works out to an annualized gain of 0.3%, hardly the stuff that you might expect would inspire a major bull market. Yet the DJIA went from a low of 197 in 1950 to a high of nearly 735 in 1961, a sizzling 272% rise.

The explanation for both markets is a steady expansion in P/E's. In 1922 the DJIA stocks had an average P/E of 10. By 1927 the figure, at above 20, had more than doubled. And during the second stage of the second secular bull market, P/E's more than *tripled,* from under 7 to over 21.

But wait a minute. I stressed earlier that the market thrives on expectations of growth. Why would investors like stocks more—as shown by the rising capitalizations they were willing to award—when growth was slowing? Isn't there a contradiction here somewhere?

Go back to our baseball analogy to understand what was happening. Once a team has established itself— once the farm system has been developed, once the credentials of the players have been proved, once the manager's skill is beyond question—a period of lackluster performance will be seen not as a disaster but as a prelude to the better times that people believe must inevitably lie ahead. That is the psychology of sports and that is the psychology of the market.

In other words, investors were confident that a period of slow growth preceded better times ahead. And, in fact, there has always been an *inverse relationship* between the fundamental and the psychological components, not just in secular bull markets but throughout market history at least as far back as 1920. Figure 9-1 summarizes the results.*

*These calculations are based on two-year averages of earnings. Thus, suppose that the Dow averaged 200 during one year and that earnings for Dow companies that year were $25 a share, while earnings were $15 a share the previous year. The P/E ratio would be calculated as 10—that is, 200/average of 15 + 25. The reason for this method is to smooth out any large fluctuations in earnings.

Figure 9-1 shows clearly that the more rapidly earnings are growing—the stronger the fundamental variable—the lower on average the P/E. *Fundamental strength begets psychological weakness, and fundamental weakness begets psychological strength.* Not, perhaps, a notion that has much applicability to personal relationships, but one that holds consistently true in the stock market.

**FIGURE 9-1**

### FOUR-YEAR EARNINGS GROWTH RATE

| Since 1920 | Average P/E |
|---|---|
| 10% or more | 12.5 |
| 5% to 9% | 12.9 |
| less than 5% | 20.0 |

What lies behind this? Plenty. The key relevant fact is that slow growth more often than not is growth with very little inflation. In other words, the psychological strength comes not so much from fundamental weakness as from very moderate inflation. And, as I have repeatedly stressed, the hallmark of a secular bull market is well-behaved inflation. Under these conditions, profits advance, but at only a moderate pace. *Only when profits are advancing at a moderate pace can investors be sure that growth is sustainable.* And when the prospects are for sustainable growth, the psychological component becomes ever more important.

Now you can see why, when corporate profits began to falter in 1984, it was *not* negative for the market,

157

though at the time many investors assumed that the result must be a major drop in stocks. Once the initial sharp spurt in profits had run its course, a slowdown in profit growth was to be both expected and desired. It was welcome evidence that this market, rather than being good only for the 100-yard dash, was in condition to run the marathon.

# Stage 3:
# Winding Down

Toward the end of the bull market, profits once again grow rapidly. But this time in the later stage of an economic expansion, circumstances have altered considerably since the first stage. Far from just recovering from recession, the economy has been growing for some time. Capacity limitations have generally been reached, companies are often overproducing, inventories are building up—and inflation is starting to rear its ugly head. *Rapid profit growth at this stage is a sign more of economic excesses than of economic stability,* and as such it is not sustainable.

Nonetheless, during this third stage, the profit growth that the economy is recording—however inherently unstable it is—does carry the market upward in a final spurt of activity. During the third stage of the first secular bull market, from 1928 through 1929, the DJIA advanced 66%. In the comparable period of the second secular bull market, 1961 to 1965, the DJIA climbed 32%. P/E's during these years fell from the low 20s to the high teens. Clearly, earnings growth was once again in control.

158

\* \* \*

What do our three stages have to tell us about how high the present market can go? We've already seen that in the first stage the DJIA gained 66%, advancing to 1295 by the start of 1984. We are now near the beginning of the second stage, in which psychology has taken over as the key element. How long will this stage last, and where will stocks be at the end of it?

Let's make a few reasonable assumptions. In 1985 the 30 Dow stocks will earn about $125 a share, and their average P/E will be about 11. Suppose earnings grow at a moderate 5% rate for the next seven years. That means that by 1992 the index will be earning $176 a share. Providing that inflation remains moderate— 4% or less a year, which I think is entirely likely—then P/E's will continue to go higher. How high? There is no automatic limit. In the past two secular bull markets the P/E of the Dow at its peak was approximately 21. Let's assume that the same figure holds in the current market. In that case, with the Dow earning $176 a share, it would mean a Dow of 3700 in the early 1990s.

But then we will still have the third and final stage to go through, in which the fundamental component takes over and earnings start to climb rapidly once again. Suppose that during the last two years of the current market, profits for the Dow were to grow by 18% to 20%. Assuming that, as in the past two secular bull markets, P/E's were to decline from 21 to around 17 or 18, we'd be left with an ultimate top between 4200 and 4500.

A Dow of 4200 to 4500. A brave projection—especially because the lion's share of the gain will come when earnings are growing at only a moderate clip, and this flies in the face of the conventional wisdom. Wall Street has its own way of valuating the market, which at first glance might seem miles apart from mine—miles apart because under standard valuation formulas, moderate earnings growth would never go hand in hand with a surging Dow. But before you send me off to the Wall Street funny farm, let's take a look at these formulas in some detail.

Every brokerage house has its own pet formula for valuating stocks, but they all revolve around two variables: *long-term interest rates* and *projected growth*. One of the better-known versions (probably because it is so inaccessible) is Goldman Sachs's equation, which goes as follows:

$$P = \frac{D \times R + [(ROE \times RE) \times (1 + G)]}{R \times R}$$

P stands for the price of whatever is being valuated, whether it be a particular stock or the DJIA. D is the dividend, R stands for long-term interest rates plus risk, and the other terms, ROE, RE, and G, all relate to estimates of growth.

This formula and others like it are based on one underlying assumption: that stock prices are positively related to growth and negatively related to interest rates. That is a fancy way of saying that when growth is expected to be high, stock prices should be high as well, while when interest rates are high, stock prices should be low. Given these assumptions, the best combination, obviously, is high growth and low rates. The worst combination is low growth and high rates, while in the middle are high growth, high rates and low growth, low rates.

Given our earlier discussion of how long-term rates are a proxy for long-term growth, you may already have spotted the flaw in this assumption—and it should come as no surprise that these complicated valuation formulas have a lousy forecasting record. Consider the following comment made in a Goldman Sachs research report at the end of August 1982: "The principal message of this evaluation framework is that the equity market has squeezed out just about all that is likely from the already large decline in bond rates. Further sustained gains in the [equity] market require lower interest rates—to provide less bond competition and allow for an earnings underpinning to share prices." The model was explicit in projecting a Dow of 1000 in about twelve months and of 1290 four years out. The projections were just a little off. The Dow reached 1000 within two months and was trading near 1290 fifteen months after the report was issued.

Or jump ahead about two years. In August 1984, with the Dow again trading near 1100, Wall Street was very glum about stocks. Institutional clients of Goldman Sachs could hardly have been much cheered by reading the following: "We believe that, point to point over the next year, the fundamental direction of share prices is down. (Obviously, this does not preclude technically based/short-term rallies.) The distillation of our valuation work . . . suggests the unfolding of large 'animal-spirited' declines (e.g. 25% or so) in share prices from current levels." Approximately two weeks later the Dow was trading in the mid-1200s, which is to say that in only ten trading days the market jumped about 13% in one of the most intense advances in market history.

I am not interested merely in pointing out that brokerage houses can be wrong; in this business anyone can be wrong. (Incidentally, a major reason I picked Goldman Sachs is that this is a particularly well regarded firm. I focused on August 1982 and August 1984 because both periods were the start of major advances that took place for reasons not accounted for by standard valuation work.) But I am interested in *why* they are wrong in such instances—in why the typical valuation model misses the boat by such a wide mark. For with this explanation comes further insight into the factors that really do propel the market—and further support for my conclusion of a Dow in the 4000s by the early 1990s.

There are two main reasons why typical valuation formulas go astray.

First, they all treat growth and interest rates as if they were completely separate—and, more often than not, inversely related—phenomena. But as you know, both these assumptions are wrong. I have shown that, over the long haul, long-term interest rates equal growth. It is worth repeating some of the evidence. Most striking is that over the past sixty-five years the average yield of long-term bonds has been 5.2%. During the same period Dow earnings have grown at an average rate of 5.2%, while asset values (book value) of the Dow stocks have grown at an average rate of 5.1%. Such statistics are compelling support for the notion that long-term interest rates reflect expectations of long-term growth. And they point up the futility of trying to relate stock prices positively to one thing (growth) and negatively to another thing (interest rates) when both things are essentially the same.

There is a second reason why standard valuation approaches to stocks completely miss the mark. Go back to the Goldman Sachs formula. There are a lot of terms in it, but not one of them represents the variable that is at least as important as anything else in valuating common stocks—and that is the *inflation rate*. Interest rates are there, growth is there, but inflation is nowhere to be found!

That may not be completely fair. After all, inflation is a part of interest rates and a part of growth. Remember, interest rates equal real growth plus inflation. But if interest rates are high does it mean that inflation is high and real growth low, or that inflation is low and real growth high, or some intermediate combination? Similarly, when interest rates are low, is it because both inflation and real growth are low, because inflation is high and growth negative, or because inflation is negative and real growth high? The point is that while bond yields are undeniably related to inflation, it is not a one-to-one relationship.

*My contention is that inflation should be more important than bond yields in determining stock valuations*—and the proof is in the data. Figures 9-2 and 9-3 summarize the relationships between P/E ratios and inflation, and between P/E ratios and AAA bond yields during the past sixty-five years.

As you can see, there is a definite relationship with respect to both variables. Which relationship is stronger? The one with inflation, clearly. When bond yields are high, P/E's are low. When inflation is high,

P/E's are also low, but even lower than when bond yields are high. Moreover, when inflation is very low, P/E's are much higher than when bond yields are low. To borrow from Reggie Jackson, inflation, not bond yields, is the straw that stirs the drink.

**FIGURE 9-2**

| Average P/E | Average Inflation |
|---|---|
| 10.20 | 9.13% |
| 16.66 | 3.88 |
| 19.63 | −.46 |

**FIGURE 9-3**

| Average P/E | Average Bond Yields |
|---|---|
| 12.05 | 9.32% |
| 23.38 | 4.18 |
| 14.80 | 3.18 |

I can take this analysis one step further. There also is a strong relationship between bonds and inflation. The real question is, if we look at bond yields apart from inflation, what is the relationship to P/E's? More precisely, does that part of bond yields that is independent, in a statistical sense, of inflation, correlate with P/E's? The answer is no—there is no such relationship. That is a strong statement and one that is worth repeating: *Bond yields in a statistical sense relate to market valuation only by virtue of the relationship between yields and inflation.* (While there are complex statistics that justify this conclusion, you can deduce the result based on what I have already said. When you take inflation out of bond yields, you end up with real rates, which are a reflection of growth, our fundamental component. And as I have already shown, the fundamental component is actually negatively related to the psychological component.)*

It is now possible to see how standard valuation formulas, when you make the right assumptions, lead us to the same place—4200 to 4500 on the Dow. Take a look at a simpler version of the Goldman Sachs model:

$$P = D/(R-G)$$

Here P equals the price of, say, the DJIA; D equals the dividend of the Dow, G stands for the projected growth rate of dividends, and R stands for what is called the *discount rate,* which is the key to the whole formula.

R appeared in the Goldman Sachs formula, too, and is the only term here which requires a bit of explanation. The discount rate refers to the return that investors require from common stocks. If stocks were perceived as being no riskier than bonds, R would equal the yield on long-term risk-free bonds. But stocks are never risk-free, and so R is always positive. Thus, $R = I + r$, where I stands for long-term interest rates and r stands for risk. The concept here is simple. If you were lending someone money, you would want to earn at least as much interest as you could get from buying a long-term bond. And the less certain you were of being

*There is one caveat. The inflation valuation relationship tends to break down during sharp economic contractions—the early 1930s is the primary example. So I should modify my conclusion to say that as long as real growth remains positive, and preferably slow rather than rapid, the level of inflation will, more than any other factor, determine how high the market is valued.

165

paid back—i.e., the greater the risk—the higher the interest rate you would charge as compensation for the additional risk. It is the same with stocks. The less sure you are of future gains with a stock, the greater r will be and the greater the difference between R and I. The key point is that R differs from I only because of the risk factor.

Let's now rewrite the above equation, using the relationship interest rates = growth: $R = I + r = G + r$.

In other words, $P = D/(r + G - G)$ or $P = D/r$. This is precisely analogous to the equation on page 152, $P = (P/E) \times E$, in that it has a fundamental component—D in one instance and E in the other case—and a psychological component, r in one case and P/E in the other case.

All you need to realize now is, first, as D goes up so does P. And what determines how fast D goes up? How fast growth is—exactly the factor that determines how fast E goes up in our original equation. Second, the lower r is, the higher P is. What determines how high or low r is? Exactly the factors I have pointed to as determining how high or low the P/E is. That is, the extent to which growth is perceived as sustainable, and that means the extent to which growth is slow but steady and inflation is low. It follows that the longer growth stays on a steady course, and the longer inflation remains low, the higher the market can go.

In other words, we have come around, by the path of standard valuation work, to my original starting point: The market is driven by a fundamental component and a psychological one. What drives the fundamental component is *growth*. What drives the psychological component is *perceived risk*, which in turn has to do with the

166

level of inflation. As long as inflation remains low, risk is perceived as low.

If you make the right assumptions, valuation analysis is completely compatible with my earlier discussion of how high this market can go.

So there you have it. No matter how you look at it, as long as you assume that inflation will remain moderate and that growth will be positive—even if very moderate—the market is headed much, much higher. Earlier, on the basis of the course of the past two secular bull markets, I offered 4200 to 4500 as my best estimate of where this one will end. But actually, when it comes to the second stage, there is no automatic limit to how much valuations will expand. It's like asking how deep is love: It is a question of psychology, not economics. P/E's will continue to climb as long as investors believe that growth is sustainable. I picked a P/E of 21 for the second stage because that was the level reached in the past secular bull markets. But if inflation remains moderate for the next ten instead of the next seven years, you might end up with a P/E of 30 or more. My projection of 4500 on the Dow would, in that case, turn out to be conservative.

But let's not get too greedy. For now I'll stick with my original projections: 4200 to 4500 on the Dow. That, I think, is still high enough to qualify as the opportunity of a lifetime.

# 10

## WHICH STOCKS?

The outlook, then, is for five to ten more years of low
inflation and steady growth, at the end of which time
the Dow will be anywhere from the high 3000s to the
mid-4000s. What steps should you be taking *now* to
ensure that you reap maximum profits?

This really involves two separate questions. First,
will stocks be the best game in town or will other investment areas prove equally rewarding? And second, if
stocks, then *which* stocks?

### Stocks, Bonds, and Other Investments

Under the economic circumstances that breed secular
bull markets, stocks unquestionably are where you can
make the greatest money, as Figure 10-1, "Annual
Rates of Return," shows. *In periods of no or low inflation,
stocks have always vastly outperformed all other types of investments.*

168

FIGURE 10-1

## ANNUAL RATES OF RETURN

|  | CPI | Stocks | Bonds | Housing | Farmland | Silver |
|---|---|---|---|---|---|---|
| **Deflation** | | | | | | |
| 1929-32 | −6.4 | −21.2 | 5.0 | −3.9 | −12.3 | −19.8 |
| **Stable Prices** | | | | | | |
| 1921-29 | −1.3 | 20.2 | 6.4 | 5.4 | −2.8 | −3.3 |
| 1934-40 | 1.0 | 12.2 | 6.2 | 0.7 | 3.9 | 1.0 |
| Average | −0.2 | 16.2 | 6.3 | 3.1 | 0.6 | 1.2 |
| **Declining & Moderate Inflation** | | | | | | |
| 1942-45 | 2.5 | 26.1 | 4.5 | 10.0 | 18.1 | −3.3 |
| 1949-65 | 2.1 | 17.5 | 2.0 | 6.1 | 8.6 | 5.2 |
| 1981-84 | 3.9 | 16.8 | 20.0 | 3.6 | −2.4 | 13.1 |
| Average | 2.5 | 20.1 | 8.8 | 6.6 | 8.1 | 5.0 |
| **Rapid Inflation** | | | | | | |
| 1940-47 | 6.8 | 12.3 | 2.6 | 12.2 | 18.5 | 8.6 |
| 1965-81 | 7.1 | 6.4 | 6.1 | 10.3 | 12.7 | 23.7 |
| Average | 7.0 | 9.4 | 4.4 | 11.3 | 15.6 | 16.2 |

*Source:* Morgan Stanley and *Investment Strategist.*

During the secular bull market of 1921–1929, for example, when prices were essentially stable, stocks had an average annual return of 20.2%, more than three times higher than the next-best choice, bonds. Similarly, from 1949 to 1965 stocks rose 17.5% a year, outperforming bonds by more than 800%. In that period the next-best investment was farmland, which appreciated at an annual rate of 8.6%.

Why do stocks outperform bonds in periods of low and moderate inflation? Over the long run, as we have seen, bond yields reflect nominal growth. This means that bond yields fall, and bond prices rise, when nominal growth falls. But during periods of price stability nominal growth tends to be relatively steady in the 5% to 8% range. This in turn means that the return on bonds is in general limited to their yields—they offer no potential for capital appreciation. By contrast, during those times stocks offer both dividends *and* the chance for big capital gains.*

During periods of deflation or rapid inflation the reverse is true. From 1965 to 1981, when prices were rising at an average rate of 7.1% a year, stocks gained only 6.4% a year, just slightly better than bonds and far worse than real estate, farmland, and silver.

*In sum, secular bull markets in stocks do not go hand in hand with secular bull markets in other investments.*

## The Best Stocks

The clear conclusion is that to make big money during the next decade you should commit yourself heart, soul, and wallet to the stock market. But which stocks? For, unlike Jonas Dowe, you are not limited to buying and

---

*The one exception is the period from 1981 to 1984, when inflation was moderate yet bonds did outperform stocks slightly. This happened because bonds were adjusting to the sharp drop in inflation, which caused yields to fall substantially. I think that this adjustment process is now mostly completed and that for the rest of this great bull market bonds will not keep pace with stocks.

selling the thirty large-capitalization stocks making up the Dow Jones Industrial Average. During the secular bull markets of the past, many stocks outperformed the DJIA by considerable margins. If the DJIA is destined to triple or more from its current level, hundreds of other stocks are likely to do even better. So, for you, the question is: Big-cap or little-cap? NYSE or OTC? High-tech or low-risk? Where do the biggest bucks lie?

Knowing how crucial growth is to the market, you might well expect me to answer: Go with the little stocks. Buy small, aggressive growth companies and watch them soar. Forget about the stodgy household names and seek out exciting small situations with the potential for outsized growth. And indeed that is part of the answer—but only part.

It comes back to the three stages of a secular bull market described in the preceding chapter. Remember that during the first and third stages the market is pro-pelled by *earnings growth*. During the long and juicy mid-dle stage, however, the market is propelled by *psychology*—by expanding P/E's. This distinction turns out to bear critically on the kinds of stocks to buy at different times during a secular bull market.

*Basically, when the driving force behind the market is rapid earnings growth—in the early and final years of the secular bull—you should concentrate on relatively small, aggressive, fast-growing companies. But during those years when the market is being pushed higher by expanding P/E's—the phase we are in now—you can do just as well or better by buying relatively safe, bigger companies, even including some of those seemingly boring household names.*

This conclusion flies in the face of conventional wisdom. Most market pros take it as an article of faith

171

that in bull markets small stocks are always the biggest winners. Indeed, the argument for small companies is a compelling one on the face of it. As long as the economy is growing, whether in an inflationary or noninflationary way, small companies will grow faster than large ones. The reason is that the smaller the base, the easier it is to generate rapid growth. It's no trick for a baby who is 7 pounds at birth to triple in size during the first year, but if a 150-pound adult puts on 15 pounds, a mere 10% increase, it is considered a major gain. A start-up company that has $5000 in sales the first year can easily keep doubling its revenues year after year; an established company with billions of dollars in sales a year can grow only incrementally.

That small is beautiful has been demonstrated time and again in relation to stocks. A good example is a study done a few years ago by a University of Chicago graduate student, Rolf Banz. Banz ranked publicly traded companies in order of total market value. He found that even after adjusting for the greater risk inherent in smaller companies, *the smallest 20% far outperformed the larger companies.**

Banz's results are summarized in Figure 10-2. They show that from 1933 to 1982, small stocks gained more than 19% a year on average, compared with less than 12% for the S&P 500 (which, as a capitalization-

---

*It is known that smaller companies tend to be more volatile than larger ones: When the market is going up, they will go up more than the average stock, and when the market is going down, they will plunge more violently. Over the past sixty-five years, despite frequent bear markets, the overall trend of stocks has been up. So if small stocks outperformed larger ones during those years, the reason could be simply their greater volatility, which would suggest that in poor markets these stocks could suffer huge losses that would negate their prior gains. But Banz found that even after factoring in the greater volatility, small stocks still outperformed big ones over the past fifty years.

172

FIGURE 10-2

## THE BANZ STUDY

| Year | Small Stocks | S&P 500 | Performance Difference |
|------|--------|---------|------------|
| 1933–37 | 35.5% | 14.3% | 21.2 |
| 1938–42 | 5.2 | 4.6 | 0.6 |
| 1943–47 | 37.8 | 14.8 | 23.0 |
| 1948–52 | 13.6 | 19.4 | −5.8 |
| 1953–57 | 11.0 | 13.6 | −2.6 |
| 1958–62 | 17.3 | 13.3 | 4.0 |
| 1963–67 | 30.2 | 12.4 | 17.8 |
| 1968–72 | 3.5 | 7.5 | −4.0 |
| 1973–77 | 8.2 | −0.2 | 8.4 |
| 1978–82 | 28.7 | 14.0 | 14.7 |
| Average | 19.10% | 11.37% | 7.73 |

weighted average, is a good proxy for large stocks). The individual five-year period that most stands out is 1973–1977, when the S&P 500 actually was down while small stocks gained a respectable 8.2%. In and of itself this period would suggest that small stocks outperform larger ones not just because they are more volatile, but because they are truly "better"—capable of growing faster.

But before you rush out and sell IBM to buy Computerwidget, or whatever, on the OTC market, take a look at the study I did of Banz's results (Figure 10-3). I analyzed his findings in terms of one additional key variable—earnings growth.

The last two lines of Figure 10-3 summarize my findings. They show that the five groups of five-year periods in which smaller stocks most outperformed larger ones were associated with average earnings growth for the market of nearly 11%. By contrast, in the remaining five periods, when earnings growth was less than 4%, large stocks did better than small ones. *When earnings growth shrinks, so does the difference in performance between large and small stocks.*

FIGURE 10-3

## THE BANZ STUDY REARRANGED
## TO SHOW THE IMPACT OF EARNINGS GROWTH

| Year | Small Stocks | S&P 500 | Performance Difference | Earnings Growth |
|------|------|------|------|------|
| 1943-47 | 37.8% | 14.8% | 23.0 | 9.3% |
| 1933-37 | 35.5 | 14.3 | 21.2 | 22.5 |
| 1963-67 | 30.2 | 12.4 | 17.8 | 8.6 |
| 1978-82 | 28.7 | 14.0 | 14.7 | 3.0 |
| 1973-77 | 8.2 | −0.2 | 8.4 | 10.9 |
| 1958-62 | 17.3 | 13.3 | 4.0 | 1.7 |
| 1938-42 | 5.2 | 4.6 | 0.6 | −1.8 |
| 1953-57 | 11.0 | 13.6 | −2.6 | 7.0 |
| 1968-72 | 3.5 | 7.5 | −4.0 | 3.8 |
| 1948-52 | 13.6 | 19.4 | −5.8 | 8.3 |
| Top 5 groups | 28.08% | 11.06% | 17.02 | 10.86% |
| Bottom 5 groups | 10.12% | 11.68% | −1.56 | 3.80% |

The reason comes back, once again, to the two forces that together drive the market: *fundamental* factors, such as dividends and earnings, and *psychological* factors, such as P/E's and risk premiums. (P/E's and risk premiums are inversely related: When P/E's are high, risk premiums are low, and vice versa.) When growth is rapid, fundamental factors are dominant, risk tends to rise, and P/E's to shrink. Under these conditions—which prevail during the initial and final stages of a secular bull market—small stocks, which are capable of sustaining the most rapid growth, benefit most. But when growth is low to moderate, as in the middle stage of a secular bull market, stocks are propelled by low risk and high P/E's. In this situation the lower risk inherent in larger companies tends to neutralize the growth advantage of smaller companies. Or to put it differently, whenever growth slows, the greater the relative risk in smaller companies.

This brings us to the present period, in which earnings growth, largely because of subdued inflation, is slowing. While this doesn't mean that small stocks will falter, it does suggest that larger companies will be able to at least keep pace with their smaller brethren—and possibly outperform them. Over the next several years you can make as much or more money in big-cap stocks as in small stocks. This should be reassuring news for those of you who sleep easier at night when the stocks in your portfolio bear such familiar names as IBM and Bristol-Myers. Only later on, in the third and final stage of this secular bull market, when P/E's will once again become the driving force behind the market, will it be time once again to emphasize smaller stocks.

175

Let's summarize our conclusions so far in Figure 10-4.

**FIGURE 10-4**

| Market Stages | Duration | Earnings Growth | Investment Choice |
|---|---|---|---|
| Stage 1 | 1–2 years | rapid | small companies |
| Stage 2 | 5–12 years | slow | large & small companies |
| Stage 3 | 2–5 years | rapid | small companies |

How would following this strategy have worked in the great secular bull market of 1949–1965? Exceedingly well, as Figure 10-5 shows. The measure of big-stock performance is once again the S&P 500; as my measure of small-stock performance I used the S&P Low-Priced Common Stocks average.

**FIGURE 10-5**

| Market Stages | Earnings Growth | Small Stocks | Large Stocks |
|---|---|---|---|
| Stage 1 (1949–50) | 11.4% | +35% | +21% |
| Stage 2 (1951–61) | 1.1 | +203 | +271 |
| Stage 3 (1962–65) | 12.9 | +39 | +29 |

The fat middle period of the current secular bull market has just begun. It is a period in which hundreds upon hundreds of stocks will easily triple or quadruple, and in which the *best* stocks may rise tenfold or more. I've shown that you don't need to be afraid of large

176

stocks during this period—that, indeed, they may be among the biggest winners. But how do you know exactly which stocks, or kinds of stocks, to pick?

I've developed three criteria. They all are geared to ferreting out companies that have the highest probability of achieving predictable and sustainable growth for at least the next five years. In an environment in which slow growth will be the norm and very rapid growth somewhat distrusted, these companies will truly stand out because of their consistently strong performance.

# 1. Criterion No. 1:
# Increasing Margins

The dramatic drop in inflation in recent years has many obvious benefits, but from the point of view of a businessperson it also has one drawback—it makes it harder to raise prices. When inflation is whipping along, price hikes are there for the taking, and all a company has to do is make sure that it is marking up its prices faster than its suppliers are increasing theirs. When inflation moderates, however, businesses must earn their money the old-fashioned way: through productivity increases, cost controls, and economies of scale. Many companies that have been pulled along by the coattails of inflation run into trouble. It isn't surprising that since 1979, operating margins for the typical industrial company have declined by about 4%, from 13.5% to 13%.

But there have been notable exceptions—companies whose margins have climbed despite low inflation. Ob-

177

viously, companies that manage to achieve this must
have a lot of good things going for them. In fact, probably no other statistic better reveals a company's underlying "right stuff" than its ability to raise margins in a
disinflationary environment. Such companies almost by
definition have much better growth prospects in disinflationary times than the average company. These are
exactly the kinds of companies you want to own.

**FIGURE 10-6**

## COMPANIES WITH RISING MARGINS
## DESPITE LOW INFLATION

| Stock | Exchange | Symbol | 5-Year Growth | % Change in Operating Margins 1979–84 |
|---|---|---|---|---|
| Abbott Laboratories | NYSE | ABT | 18% | 28% |
| American Home Products | NYSE | AHP | 12 | 18 |
| Ball Corp. | NYSE | BLL | 12 | 12 |
| Bristol-Myers | NYSE | BMY | 14 | 35 |
| Browning-Ferris | NYSE | BFI | 22 | 13 |
| Bruno's | OTC | BRNO | 20 | 59 |
| Coherent | OTC | COHR | 20 | 13 |
| Dean Foods | NYSE | DF | 21 | 44 |
| Deluxe Check Printers | NYSE | DLX | 19 | 18 |
| Dunkin' Donuts | OTC | DUNK | 17 | 14 |
| E-Systems | NYSE | ESY | 33 | 25 |
| Ennis Business Forms | NYSE | EBF | 13 | 23 |
| Genuine Parts | NYSE | GPC | 15 | 12 |
| Handleman | NYSE | HDL | 16 | 31 |

| Stock | Exchange | Symbol | 5-Year Growth | % Change in Operating Margins 1979–84 |
|---|---|---|---|---|
| Harland, John H. | NYSE | JH | 22% | 19% |
| Hartmarx | NYSE | HMX | 18 | 34 |
| Hechinger | OTC | HECH | 30 | 43 |
| Heinz, H. J. | NYSE | HNZ | 13 | 35 |
| Jostens | NYSE | JOS | 10 | 2 |
| Krueger, W. A. | OTC | KRUE | 12 | 14 |
| McDonald's | NYSE | MCD | 16 | 13 |
| Miller, Herman | OTC | MLHR | 16 | 30 |
| National Medical Enterprises | NYSE | NME | 27 | 11 |
| Philip Morris | NYSE | MO | 15 | 7 |
| Philips Industries | NYSE | PHL | 24 | 62 |
| Safety Kleen | NYSE | SK | 23 | 25 |
| ServiceMaster Industries | OTC | SMAS | 22 | 5 |
| Snap-On-Tools | NYSE | SNA | 15 | 4 |
| Thrifty | NYSE | TFD | 13 | 24 |
| U.S. Tobacco | NYSE | UBO | 20 | 27 |
| Walgreen | NYSE | WAG | 20 | 30 |
| Watkins-Johnson | NYSE | WJ | 26 | 15 |
| Weis Markets | NYSE | WMK | 15 | 21 |

Figure 10-6 presents thirty-three of these winners. Each has managed to increase its margins between 1979 and 1984, just as inflation was subsiding. For each, growth prospects are excellent for the remainder of the decade. As indicated before, many of them are large, well-known companies, from Bristol-Myers to McDonald's to Philip Morris. I would expect all of them to outperform the average stock in the next five or so years.*

## 2. Criterion No. 2:
## Making It Through Thick and Thin

The past fifteen years have been among the most turbulent in our economic history. They have included three major recessions—in 1970, 1974–1975, and 1980–1981, each in turn the most severe since the Great Depression—and one mini-recession, in 1980. It has been a period first of sharply rising prices and then of sharply decelerating inflation. In sum, these were years that required corporations to make constant adjustments to ever-changing conditions. Not surprisingly, many companies faltered at least once during this period.

Figure 10-7 lists some of those rare companies that never made a misstep. Each has posted at least fifteen consecutive years of profit growth, an extraordinary achievement. Of course, the past never guarantees the future. But any company that has so successfully negotiated the turbulent waters of the past fifteen years is a good bet to successfully negotiate the smoother sailing likely in the next decade or so. As an added check, each company in Figure 10-7 is expected to post average earnings gains of at least 10% between 1984 and 1986.

---

*A word of caution. Stock selection is an art that requires enormous flexibility at all times. While these stocks look good now, it is always possible that something unexpected could occur to change the outlook for any one of them, causing me to change my assessment.

# 3. Criterion No. 3:
# Tax Reform Winners

Wall Street likes to view itself as taking its cues from unseen economic forces and being largely independent of the machinations that take place in Washington. Most of the time this is true. One important exception, however, is likely to be President Reagan's sweeping tax reform legislation.

If we get tax reform more or less in line with Reagan's proposals, featuring lower corporate tax rates, it will mean higher reported earnings for virtually all companies, an obvious positive for stocks.* However, for some companies—the big capital-spenders—the gains will be more illusory than real, for they will be losing investment tax credits and facing longer depreciation schedules. Thus, while reported earnings will be advancing, cash flow will actually be lower. The gains will be very real, however, for companies that are not capital-intensive, because for those companies the market will push up prices so as to be commensurate with both higher earnings *and* higher cash flow.

The best examples of the latter are the service companies—especially those that have grown and should continue to grow with internally generated funds. Figure 10-8 lists some of my current favorites. They are in a wide variety of industries, from hospital maintenance to

---

* Bonds, too, are likely to be among the winners. Lower marginal tax rates for corporations as well as for individuals will reduce the incentive to borrow, as less interest will be deductible from income. At the same time lower marginal tax rates will increase the incentive to lend, as the aftertax return on money will be greater. More lenders and fewer borrowers will mean lower interest rates.

corporate employee relocation. One common denominator, however, apart from the fact that none of them is capital-intensive, is that the services they provide reduce business or consumer *costs*. As a result, each has a ready-made and growing market.

With few exceptions the stocks in Figures 10-7 and 10-8 are moderate- to large-sized companies, appropriate investments in the middle stage of a secular bull market. But when this secular bull market moves into its third and final stage, five or more years down the road, it will be time to shift into other, more speculative, issues. In this final stage the Amex and OTC should be your primary hunting grounds. Low-priced stocks with prospects for rapid earnings growth will be the truly exceptional performers.

It is also likely that at this stage speculation will start to heat up. Made complacent or greedy by the market gains that they have already reaped, investors start assuming that *rapid* growth is sustainable. Indeed, this is a definition of speculation: the combination of accelerating earnings growth and expanding P/E's. While during the third stage P/E's take a back seat to renewed earnings momentum, they do rise, especially for small companies that are experiencing the greatest growth.

In this last stage you should look for companies that purely and simply will experience the most rapid earnings growth. A glance at what happened during the third stage of the last secular bull market shows why. Earnings of Braniff Airways, for example, climbed from $.20 a share in 1962 to $1.56 a share in 1965. The price of the stock soared from a low of about 3½ in 1962 to nearly 40 in 1965. Similarly, profits of Delta Airlines

FIGURE 10-7

## COMPANIES WITH AT LEAST
## 15 CONSECUTIVE YEARS OF EARNINGS GROWTH

| Stock | Exchange | Symbol | 5-Year Growth Rate | Estimated Growth 1984–86 |
|---|---|---|---|---|
| Albertson's | NYSE | ABS | 16% | 10% |
| Bob Evans Farms | OTC | BOBE | 7 | 12 |
| Bristol-Myers | NYSE | BMY | 14 | 14 |
| Capital Cities Communication | NYSE | CCB | 17 | 14 |
| Capital Holding Corp. | NYSE | CPH | 10 | 10 |
| Community Psychiatric Center | NYSE | CMY | 34 | 25 |
| Deluxe Check Printers | NYSE | DLX | 20 | 15 |
| EG&G | NYSE | EGG | 17 | 22 |
| Emerson Electric | NYSE | EMR | 7 | 11 |
| Fleming Companies | NYSE | FLM | 14 | 15 |
| FlightSafety International | NYSE | FSI | 19 | 21 |
| Fort Howard Paper | NYSE | FHP | 13 | 15 |
| Gannett Co. | NYSE | GCI | 10 | 19 |
| Harland, John H. | NYSE | JH | 21 | 19 |
| Heinz, H. J. | NYSE | HNZ | 14 | 14 |
| Humana | NYSE | HUM | 17 | 17 |
| Jostens | NYSE | JOS | 10 | 10 |
| Kellogg | NYSE | K | 10 | 15 |
| Long's Drug Stores | NYSE | LDG | 10 | 12 |
| McDonald's | NYSE | MCD | 16 | 15 |
| National Medical Enterprises | NYSE | NME | 24 | 19 |

| Stock | Exchange | Symbol | 5-Year Growth Rate | Estimated Growth 1984–86 |
|---|---|---|---|---|
| PHH Group | NYSE | PHH | 12% | 12% |
| Philip Morris | NYSE | MO | 11 | 28 |
| RPM, Inc. | OTC | RPOW | 7 | 17 |
| ServiceMaster Industries | OTC | SMAS | 21 | 18 |
| Shoney's | OTC | SHON | 22 | 22 |
| Torchmark | NYSE | TMK | 15 | 19 |
| U.S. Tobacco | NYSE | UBO | 20 | 19 |
| Universal Leaf Tobacco | NYSE | UVV | 11 | 16 |
| Wal-Mart Stores | NYSE | WMT | 43 | 28 |
| Weis Markets | NYSE | WMK | 15 | 10 |

rose from $.81 to $2.91, as the stock climbed roughly tenfold, from a low of 8 to a high of 80. Fairchild Camera saw its profits more than triple in just one year, from 1964 to 1965; the stock zoomed from a 1964 low of about 20 a share to a 1965 high of more than 160. Finally, there was Rollins Inc., a miniconglomerate, whose profits rose more than 100% between 1962 and 1964; its share price rose more than sixfold during that same period.

Such visible, fast-growth companies will result in the biggest capital gains in the late 1980s and early 1990s. You will be able to ride these stocks comfortably during those years until any one of my four conditions falls out of place. As long as my conditions remain intact, the secular bull market will still be going strong, and stocks will continue to move higher.

FIGURE 10-8

## WELL-SITUATED SERVICE COMPANIES

| Stock | Exchange | Symbol | 5-Year Yield | Projected 5-Year Growth |
|-------|----------|--------|--------------|-------------------------|
| American Building Maintenance | NYSE | ABM | 3.3% | 13% |
| Angelica Corp. | NYSE | AGL | 2.6 | 12 |
| Equifax | NYSE | EFX | 3.7 | 15 |
| FlightSafety International | NYSE | FSI | 0.6 | 20 |
| IMS International | OTC | IMSI | 0.6 | 20 |
| Kelly Services | OTC | KELY | 1.6 | 20 |
| Olsten Corp. | ASE | OLS | 1.1 | 23 |
| PHH Group | NYSE | PHH | 2.8 | 15 |
| Parker Pen | NYSE | PKR | 2.8 | N/M |
| Premier Industrial | NYSE | PRE | 1.6 | 16 |
| Rollins Environmental Services | NYSE | REN | 4.4 | 20 |
| SafeCard Services | OTC | SFCD | — | 28 |
| Safety Kleen | NYSE | SK | 1.2 | 20 |
| ServiceMaster Industries | OTC | SMAS | 3.2 | 19 |
| Wackenhut | NYSE | WAK | 3.3 | 13 |

At some point, however, even secular bull markets must come to an end. Sometime in the early 1990s, one or more of my four conditions is almost certain to shift out of place, signifying that the long-term uptrend in the market is over and that a period of cyclical ups and downs has begun. What should you do then? It depends

185

on which condition looks wobbly. If it is condition No. 4—if the money supply starts contracting—run for the hills: Stocks will quickly become poison.

If Condition No. 2 falters first—that is, inflation is moving up to where it is more than half of bond yields—the economy may continue to grow a while longer before the bottom falls out, as was the case in 1966–1969. In fact, though the Dow in those years went nowhere, smaller stocks continued to thrive before the speculative bubble that had been building up finally burst. It is a dangerous game, but one in which you still can make money. This postsecular period, when inflation is the driving force, will favor only fast-growing, relatively low-priced stocks, under $20 a share.

Under these circumstances, the thing to watch closely is Condition No. 3, the relationship between short-term and long-term interest rates. As long as short-term rates remain comfortably below long-term rates, you can continue to make money in speculative stocks. But the instant you see the spread start to narrow, you should get out of the market.

But this postsecular bull phase is way in the future. Right now my four conditions tell us that we're still in the early years of the secular bull market itself. As long as the conditions remain in place, the opportunities are great and the risk is minimal. Happy sailing.

# INDEX

187